The Best of The Mailbox® Math—Book 2

Table of Contents

Energize your math curriculum with **The Best of** The **Mailbox® Math—Book 2**! The editors of *The Mailbox* have compiled the best teacher-tested ideas published in the 1996–2000 primary edition of the magazine to bring you this valuable, timesaving resource. Inside you'll find a wealth of math units covering all of the major mathematical topics, plus a collection of center ideas regularly featured in the magazine. A detailed table of contents makes it easy for you to locate the skills you want to teach. With dozens of fun, creative ideas that provide meaningful ways for you to strengthen students' math skills, **The Best of** **The Mailbox** *Math—Book 2* is a resource you can really count on!

www.themailbox.com

Managing Editors: Kelly Coder, Kelli L. Gowdy
Editor at Large: Diane Badden
Copy Editors: Tazmen Carlisle, Karen Brewer Grossman, Amy Kirtley-Hill, Karen L. Mayworth, Kristy Parton, Debbie Shoffner, Cathy Edwards Simrell
Cover Artist: Clevell Harris
Art Coordinator: Theresa Lewis Goode
Artists: Pam Crane, Theresa Lewis Goode, Nick Greenwood, Clevell Harris, Ivy L. Koonce, Sheila Krill, Clint Moore, Greg D. Rieves, Rebecca Saunders, Barry Slate, Donna K. Teal
The Mailbox® Books.com: Jennifer Tipton Bennett (Designer/Artist); Stuart Smith (Production Artist); Karen White (Internet Coordinator); Paul Fleetwood, Xiaoyun Wu (systems)

President, The Mailbox Book Company™: Joseph C. Bucci
Director of Book Planning and Development: Chris Poindexter
Curriculum Director: Karen P. Shelton
Book Development Managers: Cayce Guiliano, Elizabeth H. Lindsay, Thad McLaurin
Editorial Planning: Kimberley Bruck (Manager); Debra Liverman, Sharon Murphy, Susan Walker (Team Leaders)
Editorial and Freelance Management: Karen A. Brudnak; Hope Rodgers (Editorial Assistant)
Editorial Production: Lisa K. Pitts (Traffic Manager); Lynette Dickerson (Type Systems); Mark Rainey (Typesetter)
Librarian: Dorothy C. McKinney

©2003 by THE EDUCATION CENTER, INC.
All rights reserved.
ISBN# 1-56234-538-9

Manufactured in the United States
10 9 8 7 6 5 4 3 2 1

Numbers All Around!

Unearth a treasure trove of number sense with this "dino-mite" collection of easy-to-use activities!

ideas contributed by Kish Harris—Gr. 2, Southampton Academy, Courtland, VA

Extraordinary Excavation

Excavate extraordinary number awareness with this number-gathering activity. Give every student a construction paper copy of "Numbers About Me!" from page 5. Ask each child to color and personalize the booklet cover and then fold it in half. Staple a stack of 3" x 4½" blank paper inside each youngster's folded cover. Then challenge each child to unearth numbers that describe herself. Intrigue the class with an example like, "The numbers one, two, three, and four describe me. I have one nose, two thumbs, three names (first, middle, and last), and four pets." Have each child list in her booklet the numbers she unearths about herself along with a brief explanation of each. After a few days of number excavating, invite students to share a few of their findings. No doubt they'll conclude that numbers are an important part of their lives.

Roles of a Number
tells how many
tells location
tells order
measures

Discovering Purpose

This homework challenge leads students to consider the purpose of numbers. Give each student a copy of "Tracking Down Numbers" from page 5. Ask each child to list different objects in his home where actual numbers are found. Examples include a telephone, TV remote, cookbook, clock, and so on. When students return their homework, compile their findings on the board. Next, tell students that numbers serve different purposes. Display the information from "Roles of a Number" on this page and discuss each role that is listed. Then assign a different symbol to each role, and, with your students' help, use the resulting code to label each number location on the class list. Wouldn't life be confusing without numbers?

Sizing Up Numbers

Students get a real sense of number value during this large-group game. In advance, label 20 large tagboard cards with the numerals 0–9 (two cards for each number) and make student copies of the gameboard on page 6. (For a three-digit number game, make a copy of the gameboard, blacken the "Thousands" columns on your copy, and then use it to make student copies.)

To play, each student needs a gameboard and a crayon. Shuffle the game cards and stack them facedown. Challenge each student to make in the first blank row of his gameboard the largest (or smallest) number he can. Then draw a game card, say the corresponding numeral, and display the card for student reference. Wait for students to write the numeral on their gameboards before drawing another card. When six digits are recorded, ask volunteers to say the different numbers they made. Write each number on the board. When the largest possible number is identified, instruct any child who wrote that number on his gameboard to also draw two tally marks in his point box. Then shuffle the cards and begin another round of play. Play until time runs out or a predetermined number of points has been scored by one or more students.

Barbara Caywood—Gr. 3, Partridge Grade School, Partridge, KS

Number Crunching

Daily number crunching is a "dino-mite" way to strengthen students' understanding of number relationships. Every day write four different numbers on the board and give each child a copy of "Number Crunching" from page 6. Have each student copy the numbers on her paper (in the provided circles) and complete the number-crunching activities. Set aside time for youngsters to check their work as a class. Or have students compare their work with partners or with members of a small group. Crunch, crunch, crunch.

What's Hatching?

Crack open an investigation of the suitability of numbers! Explain to students that some numbers are just right for some situations, but not right for others. For example, the number 12 could be how many feet deep a swimming pool is, but could not be the number of ears on an elephant. Or the number 10 could be the number of ounces in a milk shake, but could not be the age of a school bus driver. To get students thinking about the suitability of numbers, divide the class into small groups and assign each group a different number. Challenge the members of each group to think of situations in which the number does (and does not) make sense. Then have each group use the "could be, but could not be" format to prepare two different responses for sharing with the class. After each group has shared its statements, have students work independently to complete "What's Hatching?" on page 7.

Numbers About Me!

by

_____

Tracking Down Numbers

I found numbers on these objects:

_____

_____

_____

_____

_____

_____

_____

_____

_____

_____

Note to the teacher: Use "Numbers About Me!" with "Extraordinary Excavation" on page 3. Use "Tracking Down Numbers" with "Discovering Purpose" on page 3.

5

Number Crunching

Write a different number in each circle.
Use the numbers to complete the activities below.

Write the numbers from smallest to largest.	Write 1 number 3 different ways.	Write each odd number.
Mentally add 5 to each number. Write the sums. _____ _____ _____ _____	Complete the number sentences. _____ > _____ _____ < _____	Write each even number.

Sizing Up Numbers

Point Box

ONES	ONES							
	TENS							
	HUNDREDS							
THOUSANDS	ONES							
	TENS							
	HUNDREDS							

Note to the teacher: Use "Number Crunching" and "Sizing Up Numbers" with the activities of the same name on page 4.

Name _____

Number sense

What's Hatching?

Decide what the number on each egg could and could not be.
Use the code to color the egg.

number of people in a family

6

age at which a person drives a car

number of cookies in a cookie jar

20

miles per hour at which a jet flies

length in inches of a puppy

82

degrees of temperature on a summer day

age of a school-teacher

151

number of pennies in a piggy bank

the distance in miles that a train travels

1,134

number of kittens in a litter

minutes needed to eat a hamburger

10,753

dollars needed to buy a new car

gallons of water in a swimming pool

4

number of legs on a table

number of students in a classroom

263

number of pages in a book

number of times the sun sets each day

1

number of hairs on a horse

year the safety pin was invented

1849

year the computer was invented

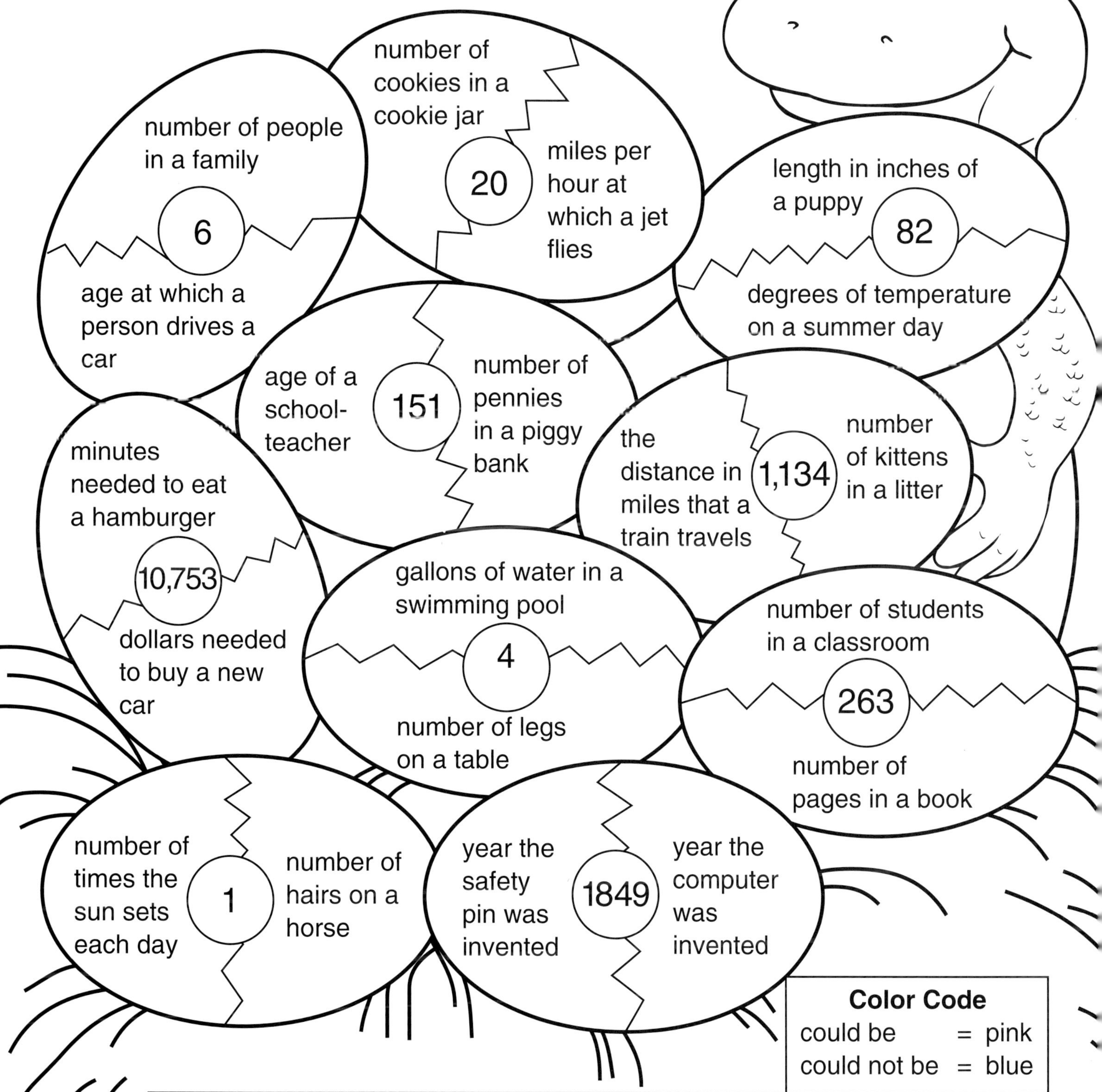

Color Code

could be = pink
could not be = blue

Bonus Box: Oops! One egg rolled away! On the back of this paper, draw a large egg and number it 12. On one half of the egg, write a phrase about the number that could be true. On the other egg half, write a phrase about the number that could not be true. Use the code to color the egg.

©The Education Center, Inc. • *The Best of* The Mailbox® *Math • Book 2* • TEC1491 • Key p. 160

Note to the teacher: Use with "What's Hatching?" on page 4.

7

THIS MUST BE THE PLACE!

Onesplace Tensplace Hundreds place Thousandsplace

Fasten your seat belt and cruise into this collection of teacher-tested, place-value activities. As you travel through the unit, you'll see that the activities can easily be adapted to meet the place-value needs of your youngsters. So what are you waiting for? The towns of Onesplace, Tensplace, Hundredsplace, and Thousandsplace await you. Grab your students and hit the road to better place-value skills!

Munchable Math

Warm up students' place-value engines with this tasty activity. Provide each student with a sandwich bag of popcorn or toasted-oat cereal and a napkin. Instruct the students to organize their snacks into groups of tens and ones. Then have each student announce the number of tens and ones she made and the total number of snack pieces she has. Conclude the activity by inviting students to munch on their snacks!

Regina Lykins—Gr. 1
Williamsburg Elementary
Loveland, OH

Place-Value Flip Chart

This handy flip chart is just what your students need to practice place value. To make a tens and ones flip chart, fold an 8½" x 11" piece of colored construction paper in half. Unfold the paper and label the halves "Tens" and "Ones" as shown. Next label ten 4" x 5" white paper cards with the numerals 0 through 9. Stack the cards in numerical order and staple the resulting card set in the ones column. Make and staple a second card set in the tens column. Place the resulting flip chart (customized to meet the place-value needs of your students) at a center for students to use with a provided place-value activity. Or assist students in creating individual flip charts. For a large- or small-group activity, announce a number and have each student display the matching number on his place-value flip chart.

Candi DeFran, East River Elementary, Grosse Ile, MI

Thousands | Hundreds | Tens | Ones
0 | 0 | 9 | 5

Barry Slate

Hurry to One Hundred

Here's a place-value game for two players that's a great addition to a math center. To make place-value blocks, laminate several sheets of half-inch graph paper; then cut the papers to create 30 one-square blocks, 30 ten-square blocks, and two 100-square blocks. (See the illustration.) Place the blocks and a pair of dice at the center. To play the game, the first player rolls the dice and collects a matching number of blocks. The second player takes his turn. When a player collects ten *ones,* he trades them for a *ten.* The first player to trade ten *tens* for a *hundred* wins the game! Ready, go!

Sue Volk, Newton, IL

Place-Value Lotto

Beep! Beep! This place-value game is sure to be a whole "lotto" fun! Write any 30 numbers from 0 to 9,999 on the chalkboard. (The numbers should reflect your students' place-value abilities.) Provide each child with a blank lotto board. Instruct him to randomly program each of the 16 squares with a different number from the chalkboard. As students are programming their cards, write the 30 posted numbers on small pieces of paper and place the papers in a container. Also give 16 paper markers to each child. To play the game, draw a number from the container and announce each digit's value. (For example, 943 would be announced as nine hundreds, four tens, and three ones.) If a student has the announced number on his board, he covers it. The first student to cover all the numbers on his board announces, "Beep! Beep!" To win the game, he must read aloud the numbers on his board for verification. If desired, award the winning student with a sticker or another small prize.

Amy Polcyn—Substitute Teacher
South Lyon Community Schools
South Lyon, MI

I Spy...Numbers!

Play this variation of the traveling game I Spy to reinforce your students' understanding of place value. To prepare for the game, ask students to pretend they're traveling on a large bus to a kid-pleasing destination like a zoo or theme park. Challenge students to name places along the way where they might see numbers. Suggestions may include license plates, highway signs, storefronts, and billboards. Next, give each child a sheet of drawing paper on which to illustrate a roadside scene. Require that each scene include a large two-, three-, or four-digit number. (If desired, provide travel magazines and brochures for drawing inspiration.) Collect the completed illustrations.

To play the game, post all (or a portion of) the roadside scenes on the chalkboard. Select one student to secretly choose a posted number. This student begins the game by announcing, "I spy a __-digit number." The rest of the students try to identify the number by asking yes-or no questions like, "Does the number have a two in the ones place?" or "Is the number greater than 500?" Stipulate that five or more place-value-related questions must be asked before the actual identity of the number may be guessed. The student who correctly names the mystery number chooses the mystery number for the next round of play. Play continues until game time is over.

Elizabeth M. Chappell—Gr. 2
Altura Elementary
Aurora, CO

Beanbag Toss

Who would guess that a beanbag toss could reinforce place-value skills? To create a four-digit gameboard, use masking tape to tape together four colorful sheets of poster board. Label the gameboard sections with place values as shown. Secure the gameboard to the floor and use masking tape to designate a toss line that is about 12 feet from one end. Divide the class into Teams A and B. Have the two teams stand on opposite sides of the gameboard—perpendicular to the toss line. Give a beanbag to each member of Team A.

To begin play, ask each member of Team A to toss his beanbag onto the gameboard (from behind the toss line). Then, with your students' help, count the beanbags that are in each place-value section and identify the four-digit number that Team A tossed. Write this number on the chalkboard. Then give the beanbags to the members of Team B and repeat the process. To determine the winner of the round, flip a penny and award a point to the deserving team: heads = the larger number tossed wins the round, tails = the smaller number tossed wins the round. If both teams toss the same number, award a point to each team. The team with the most points at the end of game time wins.

James R. McCabe—Gr. 3
Gladstone Elementary
Gladstone, OR

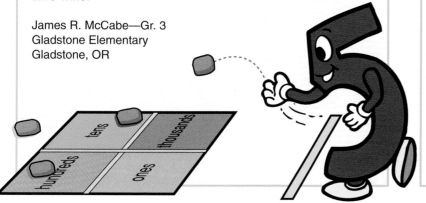

Looking at License Plates

Hit the road with this place-value project! Display a sampling of construction paper license plates that you have created.

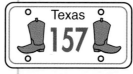

Program the plates to reflect your youngsters' place-value skills. Then ask students a series of questions related to the posted plates like, "Which license plate has an even numeral in the hundreds place?" and "Which license plate has less than three tens?" Conclude the large-group activity by enlisting the students' help in arranging the license plates in numerical order from the smallest to the largest numbers.

To extend the activity, ask each student to design a colorful license plate on a 6" x 12" rectangle of drawing paper. Then place the students in small groups and challenge each group to create a predetermined number of place-value questions about its group's license plates. Make plans for each group to present its resulting place-value lesson to the rest of the class!

Elizabeth M. Chappell—Gr. 2
Altura Elementary
Aurora, CO

Bus Bonanza

This unique activity provides busloads of place-value practice! Create three large school-bus cutouts. Label the cutouts as shown and laminate them for durability. Also program a class set of blank cards with numbers from 0 to 999. Write the numbers at the bottom edge of the cards and underline one digit per number. Pass out the numbered cards and ask each child to draw and color a self-portrait on his card. When the drawings are complete, display each bus cutout in a different classroom location. In turn, have each child read aloud the number on his resulting passenger card, identify the value of the underlined digit (ones, tens, or hundreds) and place the card on the corresponding bus cutout. Next, have the students gather around the bus cutouts they "boarded" and work together as a group to sequence the passenger cards—placing the smallest number at the front of the bus and the largest number at the back.

Later, laminate the passenger cards; then place the cards and bus cutouts at a math center for more place-value reinforcement. All aboard!

Elizabeth M. Chappell

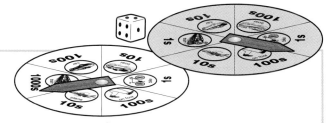

Going Places!

Students accumulate travel miles as they play this small-group place-value game! Each group needs a programmed spinner to play. To make a master spinner for duplication, photocopy page 12; then cut out the spinner labels and glue them on the spinner wheel. Program each wheel section with a desired place value (ones, tens, etc.); then make construction paper copies of the wheel and spinner patterns. Laminate the copies for durability if desired. To assemble the spinners, refer to the directions at the bottom of page 12.

To play the game, divide students into small groups. Each group member needs a sheet of paper and a pencil. Each group needs a die and a spinner. If desired, a calculator can also be provided. In turn, each group member spins the spinner to determine his method of travel and its place value. Then he rolls the die to determine how far he travels. For example, if a student spins a car (with a place value of tens) and he rolls a 6, he travels "six tens," or 60 miles. As soon as the player records his travel miles on his paper, the next player takes his turn. Play continues in this manner. When a player takes his second turn, he records his travel miles and finds the sum of miles he has traveled so far before the next player takes his turn. The first player to travel 200 miles (or another predetermined number) wins the game.

Elizabeth M. Chappell—Gr. 2
Altura Elementary
Aurora, CO

Read It!

Place-value practice takes on a new dimension with this partner game. To make the game, duplicate pages 12 and 13 on tagboard. Cut out 33 construction paper game cards (2½" squares). Label six of the cards "0." Stack these cards facedown on the gameboard (page 13) where indicated. Label the remaining cards with the numerals 1 through 9—three cards per numeral. Shuffle these cards and place them facedown on the gameboard where indicated. To make a spinner for the game (page 12), program two sections of the wheel with the words "Read It!" Program the remaining wheel sections with the following place values: "ones," "tens," "hundreds," "thousands." To assemble the spinner, refer to the directions at the bottom of page 12. To play the game, the partners (in turn) spin the spinner to determine a place value, draw a numeral card, and place the card on the corresponding gameboard space. A player may stack his numeral card atop another numeral card to make his play. The first person to spin "Read It!" places a "0" card on each open gameboard space and reads the resulting number. If the number is read correctly, the player earns one point; the gameboard is cleared; the cards are sorted, shuffled (as needed), and stacked; and another round of play begins. If a number is read incorrectly, the zero cards are removed and play continues. If all the gameboard spaces are covered before a player spins "Read It!," the player who covers the last gameboard space reads the number for a possible point. The player with the most points at the end of game time wins!

Jacqueline L. Jerke—Chapter 1 Reading and Math
Wynot Public Schools
Wynot, NE

Making Numbers

This whole-group activity provides plenty of place-value practice. Give each student ten squares of white paper. Have each child label her squares with the numerals 0 to 9. To begin the activity, announce two or more different numerals. Instruct each student to use her numeral cards to make the smallest (or largest) number possible. If three or more numeral cards are being used, also challenge students to use the numerals to make as many numbers as possible. No doubt students will ask for this hands-on activity over and over again!

Elizabeth M. Chappell

Patterns for Making a Spinner

Use with "Going Places!" and "Read It!" on page 11.

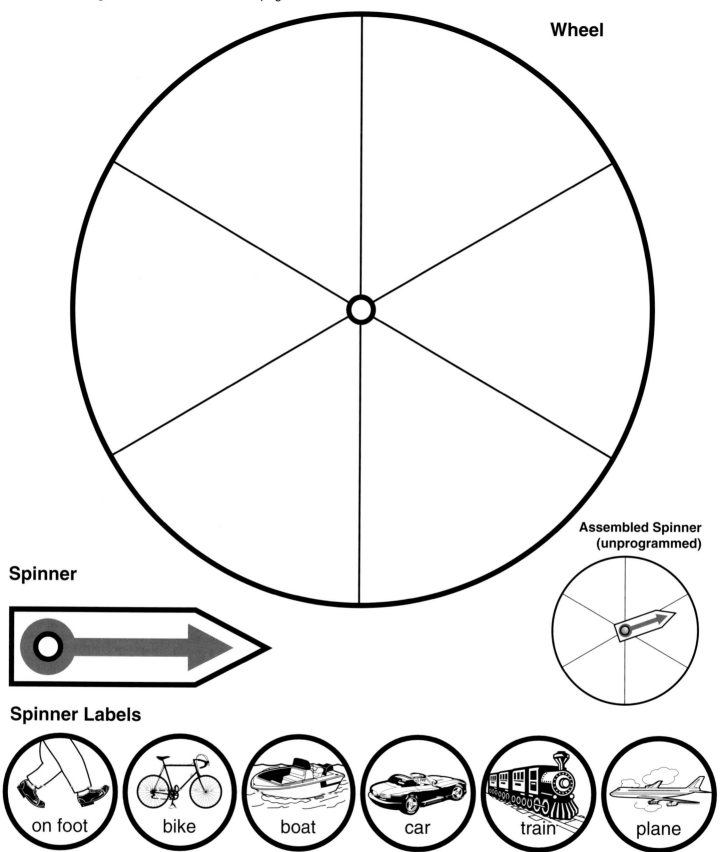

Wheel

Spinner

Assembled Spinner (unprogrammed)

Spinner Labels

on foot · bike · boat · car · train · plane

How to Assemble the Spinner: Cut out the duplicated wheel and spinner patterns. (Be sure to follow the programming directions provided in the corresponding ideas on page 11.) Punch a hole in each cutout where indicated and use a brad to join the cutouts as shown above.

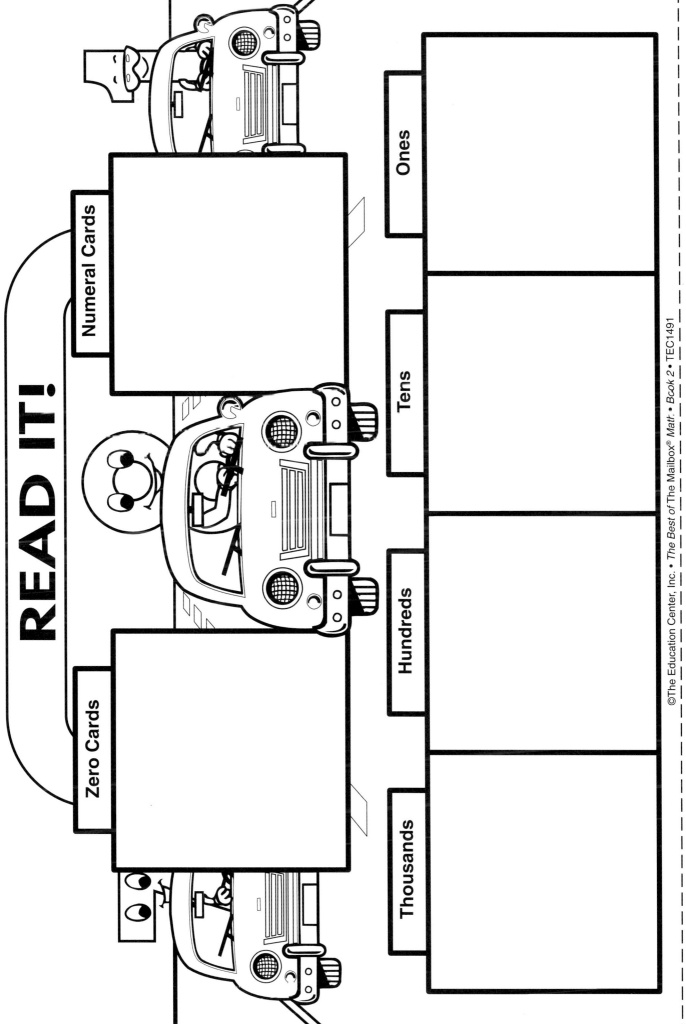

READ IT!

Numeral Cards

Zero Cards

Thousands	Hundreds	Tens	Ones

Note to the teacher: Use with "Read It!" on page 11.

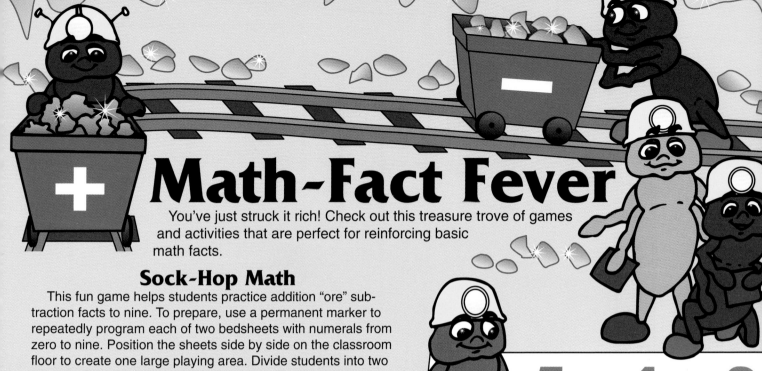

Math-Fact Fever

You've just struck it rich! Check out this treasure trove of games and activities that are perfect for reinforcing basic math facts.

Sock-Hop Math

This fun game helps students practice addition "ore" subtraction facts to nine. To prepare, use a permanent marker to repeatedly program each of two bedsheets with numerals from zero to nine. Position the sheets side by side on the classroom floor to create one large playing area. Divide students into two groups. Have the members of each group stand in their stocking feet on opposite sides of the playing area, facing each other. Give red construction paper squares to the members of one group. Give blue construction paper squares to the members of the other group.

Begin play by calling out a math fact. Each student calculates the answer, then attempts to locate and stand on that answer in the playing area. Since only one student may occupy a numeral, students who do not locate the appropriate numeral return to the sidelines. When the activity has subsided, call out the answer. If a student is standing on the right answer, he holds up his construction paper square. The team that holds up the most construction paper squares earns one point. Then have all students return to the sidelines and begin another round of play.

Kristin McLaughlin—Substitute Teacher
Boyertown Area School District
Boyertown, PA

Addition Tic-Tac-Toe

Names: John D. & Tina

Game #1

2	9	12
4	6	10
11	8	5

Game #2

9	7	2
4	8	11
12	3	6

Game #3

2	12	7
8	4	10
6	9	5

Game #4

10	4	7
9	5	2
6	3	11

Basic Fact Tic-Tac-Toe

Who would guess that playing tic-tac-toe could reinforce basic fact knowledge? To play this partner game, a twosome needs two pencils, two dice, and a duplicated gameboard. To make a gameboard, draw four or more blank tic-tac-toe grids on a sheet of paper; then program each grid with nine fact answers that can be derived by adding, subtracting, or multiplying the numbers on a pair of dice. (For example, to reinforce addition, only answers from 2 through 12 would be suitable.) Add a title and number each grid; then duplicate the completed gameboard. To play a game of addition tic-tac-toe, one partner rolls the dice and determines the sum of the numbers shown. If the answer is on the appropriate tic-tac-toe grid, he draws his assigned symbol (*X* or *O*) atop it and his turn is over. If the answer is not on the grid, the player's turn is over. Play alternates back and forth in this manner until the game is completed. A player earns a point for each game he wins. If the game is a draw, both players earn a point.

Laurie Albanos—Gr. 3, Powers Ferry Elementary School, Marietta, GA

Make Ten

Deal up some fun with this addition game for four players. Before play begins, remove all face cards from a deck of playing cards. One player deals five cards to each player. Then he lays one card faceup on the playing surface *(discard pile)* and stacks the rest of the cards facedown *(chance pile)*. The object of the game is to make sums of ten. Aces are worth one point each.

The player to the left of the dealer takes his turn first. This player checks his hand for sums of ten. If the player has card(s) that total ten, he lays them faceup on the playing surface in front of him, then discards one card from his hand and his turn is over. If a player has no cards to lay down, he takes the top card from the discard pile or the chance pile. If this new card creates a sum of ten, he lays down the appropriate card(s); then he discards one card from his playing hand. If he has no cards to lay down, he simply discards one card from his hand. The winner of the game is the first player to have no cards at the end of his turn.

Judy Bauer, Burton Elementary School
Huntington Woods, MI

Card-Game Challenge

Hit pay dirt with this five-player card game! Explain that each player's goal is to have the highest value of cards in her hand when the round is over. (Face cards are worth ten points and aces are worth one point.) To begin, one player deals four cards to each player. Then she lays one card faceup on the playing surface *(discard pile)* and stacks the rest of the cards facedown *(chance pile)*.

The player to the left of the dealer takes her turn first. This player identifies the card in her hand that has the lowest value. She then has three choices: 1) She may pass, which means she likes all of her cards. 2) She may take the top card in the discard pile, then discard a card of lesser value. 3) She may take the top card in the chance pile and then discard the lowest card in her hand. After all players have taken their turns, each player adds up the numbers on her cards. The player with the largest sum earns a point for the round. Play continues in this manner for a desired number of rounds. The player with the most points at the end of the game wins.

Doris M. Hautala—Gr. 3, Washington Elementary School
Ely, MN

Sum It Up

This small-group addition game is a "lode" of fun! Before play begins, remove the face cards and aces from a deck of playing cards; then stack the remaining cards facedown on a playing surface. To play, the first of four players selects three playing cards from the pile, turns them over, and adds the numbers printed on the cards. He announces his answer to the group, and the other players verify his calculations. To complete the round, the remaining players repeat this process. At the end of the round, students determine which player had the highest sum and which player had the lowest sum. Play continues for as many rounds as desired. As students become more proficient, challenge them to select four, five, or six cards from the pile and add the numbers together.

Jill VanDerveer—Gr. 1, Rockland Elementary, Libertyville, IL

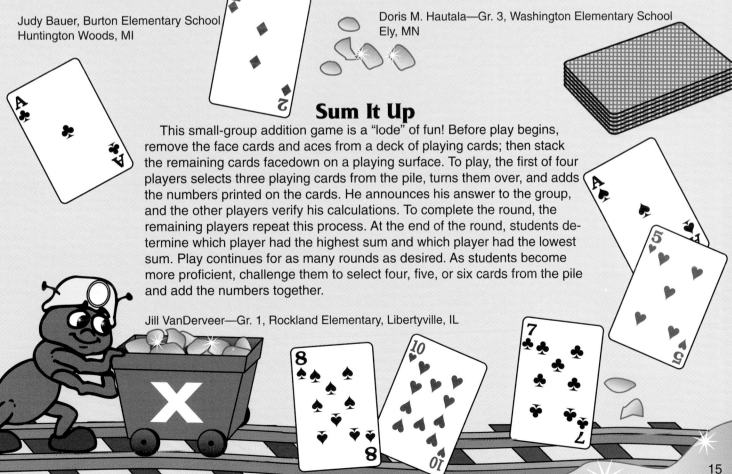

Picture a Product

Being able to visualize multiplication facts makes learning them a "hole" lot easier. And these fact bags can do just that! To make a fact bag, label the outside of a resealable plastic bag with the appropriate fact, such as "x 4." Then use a hole puncher to punch each of 10 or 12 cards with four holes. Store the cards in the bag. Place the bag and a set of "x 4" flash cards at a center. A student chooses a flash card and then uses the hole-punched cards to help her visualize and solve the multiplication fact.

Sue Warrington—Gr. 2, South School, Kennett, MO

Start to Finish

This fast-paced game helps students practice their basic math facts. Draw a series of boxes on the board as shown. Program each box with a sum, a difference, a product, or a quotient. Then ask each student to quickly write a math fact that corresponds with each answer. As soon as a student finishes, she puts her pencil down. After each student has finished, ask students to name the different facts that they printed for each answer.

Gina Naseef—Gr. 2, SS Clement-Irenaeus, Philadelphia, PA

Start
1. 6 2. 24 3. 18 4. 12 5. 30 6. 15 7. 10 Fini 8. 36

Name Cole
Start to Finish!
1. 2 x 3
2. 6 x 4
3. 6 x 3
4. 4 x 3
5. 6 x 5
6. 5 x 3
7. 2 x 5
8. 6 x 6

Memory Math

Committing math facts to memory is no "miner" task! Help students learn their facts by playing Memory Math—a Concentration-type game. Each pair of students needs a set of ten or more fact cards and a set of corresponding answer cards. (Duplicate the fact cards and the answer cards on different colors of construction paper.) To play, one student shuffles the fact and answer cards; then she places each card facedown on a playing surface. In turn, each player turns over one fact card and one answer card. If the cards match, the player keeps the cards and turns over two more. If the cards don't match, the player turns them facedown again. Play continues in this manner until all the cards have been matched. The player with the most cards at the end of the game wins.

Laurie Albanos—Gr. 3, Powers Ferry Elementary School, Marietta, GA

Multiplication Sundae Treats

Motivate students to learn their multiplication facts with this delicious idea. Give each student a white construction paper copy of the sundae pattern on page 18. Ask each child to keep this paper in a folder or notebook inside his desk. After testing the students on their knowledge of multiplication facts for zero and one, allow each student who passes the test to color in the sundae dish on his paper. Repeat this process for multiplication facts for two, three, four, and five, and have the student color the sundae pattern as indicated. Retest at each fact level as needed. After all students have completed their sheets, reward them with a sundae party. If desired, staple the finished projects to a bulletin board titled "Multiplication Is Deliciously Easy."

Debbie McGinnis—Gr. 3, Maplecrest School, Lebanon, MO

Name Tim Brody

You're in the Hot Seat!

The sentence "You're in the hot seat!" usually means trouble. But during this fun math game, you'll have students begging to be in the hot seat. Before playing, write approximately 20 fact problems (with answers) on the chalkboard. Near one end of the chalkboard, draw a large star. Ask one volunteer to sit in the hot seat (a chair) with his back to the chalkboard and ask another volunteer to be the recorder. In turn, students appointed by the recorder ask the child in the hot seat to solve a math fact from the chalkboard. If the child answers correctly, he earns one point (which is tallied by the recorder) and is given another fact problem to answer. If he can correctly answer five fact problems in a row, he writes his name under the star on the chalkboard and becomes the recorder. Then a different volunteer takes the hot seat. If the student in the hot seat misses a fact, he returns to his seat and waits for another turn. To increase the pace and difficulty of the game, establish a time limit for each answer.

Janette E. Anderson—Grs. K–3 Substitute Teacher, Fremont Unified School District, Fremont, CA

"Facts-a-thon"

How can you boost enthusiasm for learning math facts and collect much-needed classroom supplies at the same time? Hold a "Facts-a-thon!" To gather pledges for the event, duplicate the pledge sheet (and parent letter) on page 19. Program each box in the event column with a different math activity that students will complete during your classroom "Facts-a-thon." Program each donation box with an inexpensive classroom supply such as a button, a used children's book, a fabric scrap, a paper-towel tube, or a small box of tissue. In the parent letter, write the date by which you would like the pledge sheets returned; then sign the letter. Duplicate a class supply of the programmed page and have each student take home a copy for his parent(s).

Keep the returned pledge sheets handy. After each "Facts-a-thon" event, initial the appropriate pledge sheets. When your classroom "Facts-a-thon" has been completed, send all initialed pledge sheets home with the appropriate children so that the pledges can be fulfilled.

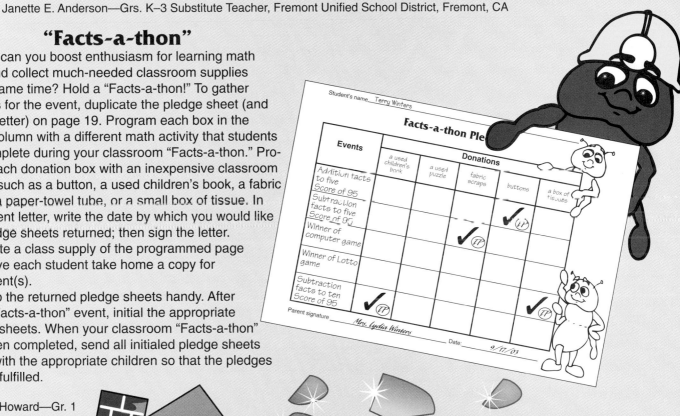

Marsha Howard—Gr. 1
First Baptist Church
Athens, TX

One of the Family

Have some "family" fun with this math activity. In advance program each of four index cards with addition and subtraction problems for a given fact family. Repeat this process for several fact families until you have one card for every student. Then, for each fact family, cut a house shape from a sheet of 12" x 18" construction paper. To begin, pass out the cards. Ask each youngster to find the other members of his fact family and sit down with them in a group. Next, give each group a house-shaped cutout. Have one member from each group program the roof area with the three numbers in the group's fact family. Then have each group member glue his index card to the group cutout so that it creates a window in the house. Also provide time for the students in each group to add colorful details to their fact houses. Display each group's work on a bulletin board titled "One of the Family."

Juanita Hytry—Gr. 1, St. Paul School, Mosinee, WI
Diane Ivey—Gr. 2, Elcan-King Elementary, Bainbridge, GA

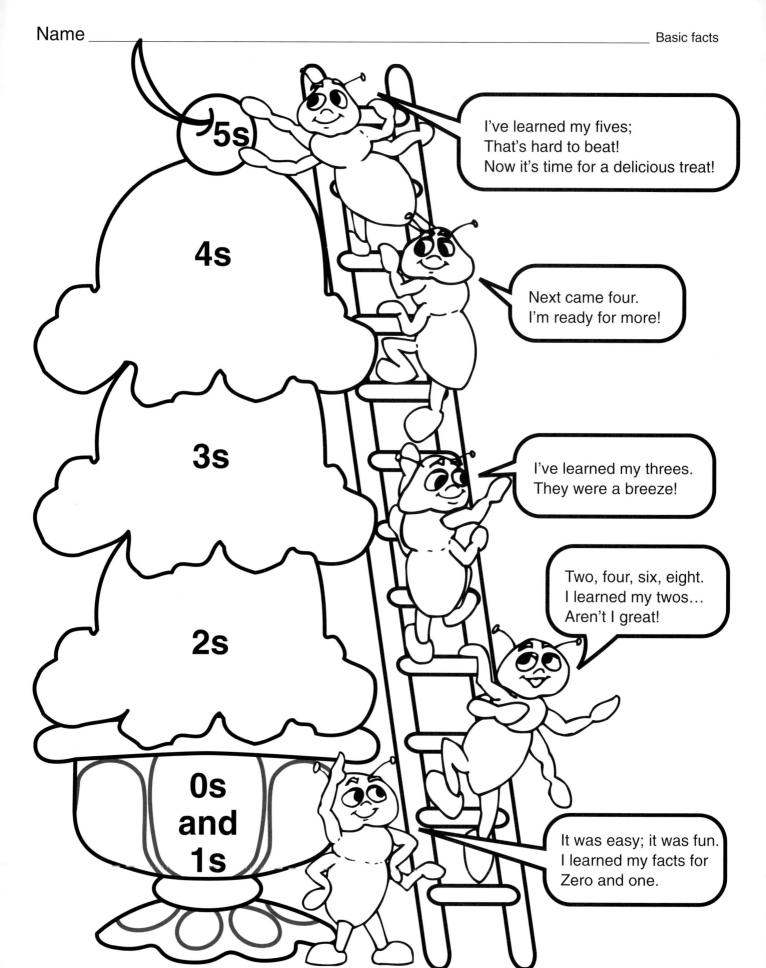

Note to the teacher: Use with "Multiplication Sundae Treats" on page 16.

Dear Parent,

During the next several weeks, your child will be participating in a classroom "Facts-a-thon." This event is a fun way for your child to practice his math facts, and it also helps our class collect supplies that we will use during the school year.

Your child will participate in each event listed on the pledge sheet below. You may sponsor him in any event(s) that you choose. To make a pledge for an event, decide which donation you would like to make if your child meets the established criterion, and mark the appropriate box. Then sign, date, and return the pledge sheet to school by _____.

(date)

Please do not send any pledged items at this time. At the conclusion of our classroom "Facts-a-thon," your child will bring home his pledge sheet. At that time you may send in each donation that I have initialed.

Thank you for your help!

Sincerely,

- -

Student's name_____

Facts-a-thon Pledges

Events	Donations				

Parent signature_____ Date _____

Take It to the Bank!

Plan to cash in on this high-interest math activity where each student hones his addition and subtraction skills by managing a just-for-fun checking account!

idea by Denise Zonder and Joanne Kokoszka—Gr. 3, Isbister Elementary, Plymouth, MI

Getting Started

Mention making checkbook covers and your young tycoons will be all ears! To make a checkbook cover, fold up the bottom two inches of a 9" x 12" sheet of tagboard and staple each end of the folded flap to make a pocket. Cut out a copy of the checkbook register (on page 21) and staple it to the top of the tagboard as shown. Next, fold the tagboard just below the register, keeping the pocket to the inside, and then fold down the top of the project. Allow time for each child to personalize and decorate his checkbook cover as desired.

Checks for the Checkbook

For a one-week checkbook project, give each child five blank checks (pattern on page 21). Have each child cut out his checks, number them from 1 to 5, and store them in sequential order in the pocket of his checkbook.

Getting Started

Talk with students about how a checking account works, including the definitions of *deposit* and *balance*. Then have each student enter the same deposit in his check register. For example, suggest a $500.00 deposit if students are regrouping over zeros or a $99.99 deposit if students are not yet regrouping. To add to the fun, tell students that the money is a gift from your great-aunt Moneybags.

Next, announce that the electric bill is due on the spot! Have each child remove check number 1 from his checkbook and write his name in the top left-hand corner. Demonstrate how to write this check, and have each child write his check in the same manner. Next, show how to enter the check amount in the check register and how to calculate the account balance. Have students do the same. Verify that everyone's account balance matches. Quickly evaluate the written checks; then have each child store his written check at the back of his checkbook pocket.

Daily Transactions

Each morning, write directions on the chalkboard for paying a bill or making a purchase (see "Sample Transactions" for ideas). Occasionally notify the class that Great-Aunt Moneybags has sent money and a deposit is in order. Before the end of each day, evaluate the checks the students have written and help them agree on a current account balance.

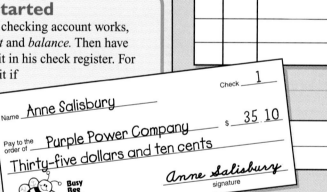

Check Number	Date	Description	Amount of Check	Amount of Deposit	Balance
	6/7	Money from Great Aunt Moneybags		99.99	$ 99.99
1	6/7	Purple Power Company	$35.10		35.10 / $ 64.89
					$.
					$.
					$.
					$.
					$.
					$.
					$.
					$.

Check **1**

Name **Anne Salisbury**

Pay to the order of **Purple Power Company** $ **35.10**

Thirty-five dollars and ten cents

Busy Bee Bank

Anne Salisbury
signature

2

Closing the Account

When the final check is written and the account is balanced, inform students that it's time to close the account. For a fun writing extension, have each child write and illustrate a paragraph describing how he plans to spend his account balance (be sure it's generous). Post these projects on a bulletin board titled "Show Me the Money!" Then send your budding bankers home with their completed checks and balanced checkbooks. Won't their parents be impressed?

Sample Transactions
- Pay the phone bill so Great-Aunt Moneybags can continue to call!
- Buy a computer game at Computers Are Cool.
- Buy pizza and soft drinks for your family.
- Pay the doctor bill. Someone ate too much pizza!
- Donate money to the local animal shelter.

20

Patterns

Use with "Take It to the Bank!" on page 20.

Check Number	Date	Description	Amount of Check	Amount of Deposit	Balance
					$.
					.
					$.
					.
					$.
					.
					$.
					.
					$.
					.
					$.
					.
					$.
					.
					$.
					.
					$.
					.
					$.

Check _____

Name _____

Pay to the
order of _____ $_____ . _____

Busy Bee Bank

_____
signature

THE MULTIPLICA

Keep your youngsters' multiplication skills on course with these teacher-tested maneuvers!

Need Ideas for Reinforcing Addition and Subtraction Facts?
Look for this symbol (✱) at the end of an activity. These ideas can easily be adapted for this purpose.

Stamping Sets

Steer students to a picture-perfect understanding of multiplication with Crayola Washable MiniStampers! Give each child a ministamp marker to keep as her own, or keep a class supply on hand. For a large-group activity, announce individual multiplication facts. A student writes the fact on her paper. Then she uses a marker and her pencil to create the corresponding set or sets before she writes the fact answer. Encourage students to use this technique when working independently too. Vroom!

Anne Fuchs—Grs. K–2 Title I, Rosemount Elementary
Rosemount, MN

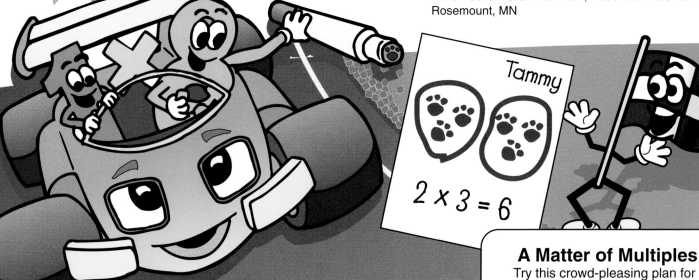

Colorful Beadwork

Need to refuel your youngsters' understanding of multiplication sets? Try this colorful hands-on approach! Every student needs a pipe cleaner and access to a supply of colorful craft beads. First, have each child knot one end of his pipe cleaner. Then have each student thread beads onto his pipe cleaner to show the set(s) associated with a specified fact. For example, to show "2 x 3," a student might thread three red beads onto his pipe cleaner, followed by three blue beads. Then have the students announce the product of the fact before they remove the beads from their pipe cleaners and await the next fact. Continue in this manner for as long as desired. Confusion over multiplication sets will be a thing of the past—and that's a fact!

Vicki Kulp—Gr. 3
Bushkill Elementary School
Nazareth, PA

A Matter of Multiples

Try this crowd-pleasing plan for reinforcing multiples! Each day for math warm-up, play a game of Secret Number. To play, draw a line on the chalkboard. Write a number to the left of the line; then write a greater number to the right of the line. Explain that the secret number is between these two numbers. Also tell what the secret number is a multiple of. Then have students ask questions about the number's identity. Require that each question include a multiple of the provided multiple. For example, if the secret number is a multiple of four, a student might ask, "Is the number between 12 and 24?" or "Is the number greater than 28?" When the secret number is identified, the game is over. Mastering multiples will make memorizing multiplication facts a breeze!

Trisha Owen—Gr. 3
Libbey Elementary School
Wheatland, WY

Communicating Commutative Property

Take the illusion out of commutative property at this pit stop! Tell students that the product of a multiplication fact stays the same when the factors are reversed. To prove your point, have each child trim a 9" x 12" sheet of black construction paper into the shape of a magician's hat. Then give each child 12 animal crackers. Write "3 x 4" on the chalkboard and instruct students to arrange their manipulatives into three groups of four crackers each on their hats. Then write "4 x 3" on the chalkboard and have the students use the same manipulatives to form four groups of three crackers each. Presto—it's the same product! Repeat the exercise, using other facts having products of 12 or less. Then, for the ultimate vanishing act, invite each student to eat his math manipulatives. Hey, that's zero times zero!

Rebecca Brudwick—Gr. 1
Hoover Elementary School
North Mankato, MN

In the Cards

Spark additional interest in fact practice with this partner game. Remove the face cards and aces from a deck of playing cards; then store the remaining cards at a center. To play, one partner shuffles the cards and places them facedown on the playing surface. Then, in turn, each partner draws two cards from the stack and places them faceup. Next, each partner announces the product of his two cards. The student with the highest (or lowest) product wins the round and keeps all four cards. If the players' products are equal, each partner draws one more card. Then he multiplies the numerals from two of his cards to create the highest (or lowest) possible product. The player who wins the round keeps all six cards. The game is over when one player holds all the cards! *

Jolene DuBose—Gr. 2
A.T. Mahan Elementary School
Keflavik, Iceland

Pass It Along!

This fact review is a ball of fun and speedy too! In advance, use a permanent marker to randomly label an inflated beach ball with numerals from 0 to 10. To play, have students quickly line up single file. Toss the ball to the first person in line. When this student catches the ball, he reads aloud the factor that is closest to each thumb in the form of a multiplication problem and then answers the problem out loud. As soon as his answer is approved by you, he quickly passes the ball between his legs (or over his head) to the student behind him. This student repeats the procedure. When the last person in line answers his problem, he tosses the ball to you. Store the ball for later use. Plan to play this fast, fun, and factual review one or more times a week! *

Dawna Salldin—Gr. 3
Wadsworth Elementary School
Palm Coast, FL

Barry Slate

Daily Lotto

A daily practice lap of lotto is a surefire way to reinforce multiplication facts! Have each child store in her desk a zippered bag that contains paper markers and a laminated lotto card of fact answers. Each day, begin math by announcing the lotto game of the day (like Blackout, Four Corners, Four in a Row, etc.). When the students are ready to play, write individual fact problems on the overhead or chalkboard. If the problem's product is on a student's lotto board, she covers it with a paper marker. The first student to cover the lotto spaces needed to win the game announces "Lotto!" Reward the winner of each day's game with a seasonal sticker. This daily practice is sure to help students memorize their facts! *

Nicole Weber—Grs. 2–3, Waterloo Elementary School
Waterloo, WI

23

Oops! Oh well...

Multiplication Basketball

Speed and accuracy count when it comes to this fast-paced fact game! All you need to play is a set of multiplication flash cards, an empty wastepaper basket, and a small rubber ball. Divide students into two teams. After asking one member from each team to stand, display a flash card. The student who is first to provide the correct answer earns one point for his team and a shot at the basket. If the player shoots the rubber ball into the wastepaper basket, he earns two more points for his team. Choose two different players for the next round of play. Continue playing until every child has participated at least once. The team with the most points at the end of game time wins! ✷

Sonya Huss—Gr. 1
Windsor Woods Elementary
Virginia Beach, VA

A Piece of Cake!

Your young drivers will be eager to prove that multiplication is a piece of cake—especially when their efforts are rewarded with cake! As soon as each child masters a predetermined number of multiplication factors (for example, factors through five), ask a parent volunteer to bake and frost a large sheet cake for the students. For added fun, suggest that the parent volunteer cut the cake into serving-size portions, and use decorating gel to program each portion with a multiplication fact. When the cake is served to the class, you can count on each student to answer his fact *and* eat his cake too! ✷

adapted from an idea by Debbie Lerner—Grs. 1–3 Multiage
Red Bridge Elementary
Kansas City, MO

WINNER'S CIRCLE

Tasty Motivation

Entice students to memorize multiplication facts with the promise of a taco party. How does this plan work? The students, working at their own pace, earn party refreshments by mastering their multiplication tables! Program a copy of "Taco Party!" on page 25 with a party date; then duplicate a class supply of the form. Have each child personalize his form and keep it in his math folder or another designated location. Each time a child shows mastery of a times table, date and sign his form. On the day of the party, each child enjoys the refreshments he has earned. Now, that's a "taco-rific" plan! ✷

Shannon Jones—Gr. 3, John Redd Smith Elementary
Collinsville, VA

Ready, Set, Multiply!

Use the handy form on page 25 to create an individualized speed-drill program. First, program a copy of the form for each factor, zero through ten (or 12). Do this by writing the factor in the star on the car. Then duplicate a supply of each programmed form and file it in an individual folder labeled with the corresponding factor. Each child begins the program with factor zero. Each time a student shows mastery of a factor, he progresses to the next higher factor. To take a speed drill, a student revs up his engine by first writing the car's number in each circle. Then he waits patiently for a starting signal from you. When the signal is given, he answers as many facts as he can in the time allotted. Ready, set, multiply!

Name _____

Taco Party!

Memorize your facts!
Earn a taco and more!

The party will be _____

Fact	Party Item	Signature	Date Mastered
x 0	cup		
x 1	drink		
x 2	paper plate		
x 3	taco shell		
x 4	meat		
x 5	napkin		
x 6	lettuce		
x 7	tomatoes		
x 8	cheese		
x 9	ingredient of your choice		
x 10	chips and salsa		

Name _____

Ready, Set, Multiply!

Answer each fact.

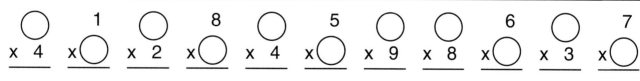

$\bigcirc$ 1
x 4   x $\bigcirc$

$\bigcirc$ 8
x 2   x $\bigcirc$

$\bigcirc$ 5
x 4   x $\bigcirc$

$\bigcirc$
x 9   x 8

$\bigcirc$ 6
x $\bigcirc$ x 3

$\bigcirc$ 7
x $\bigcirc$

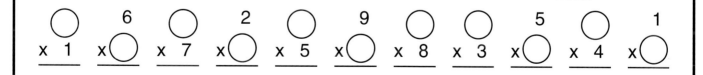

$\bigcirc$ 6
x 1   x $\bigcirc$

$\bigcirc$ 2
x 7   x $\bigcirc$

$\bigcirc$ 9
x 5   x $\bigcirc$

$\bigcirc$
x 8   x 3

$\bigcirc$ 5
x $\bigcirc$ x 4

$\bigcirc$ 1
x $\bigcirc$

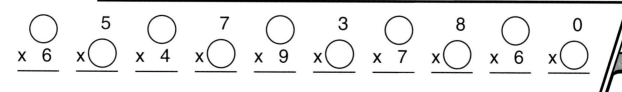

$\bigcirc$ 5
x 6   x $\bigcirc$

$\bigcirc$ 7
x 4   x $\bigcirc$

$\bigcirc$ 3
x 9   x $\bigcirc$

$\bigcirc$
x 7   x 6

$\bigcirc$ 8
x $\bigcirc$

$\bigcirc$ 0
x $\bigcirc$

Note to the teacher: Use the taco incentive plan with "Tasty Motivation" on page 24. Use the speed-drill form with "Ready, Set, Multiply!" on page 24.

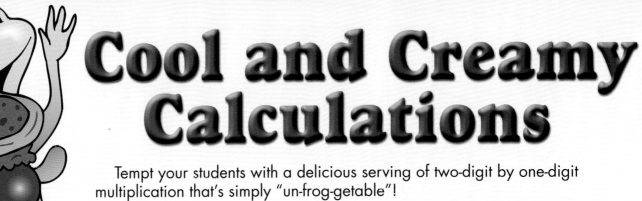

Cool and Creamy Calculations

Tempt your students with a delicious serving of two-digit by one-digit multiplication that's simply "un-frog-getable"!

ideas contributed by Danielle Conforti—Gr. 3, Old Mill Elementary School, Sea Girt, NJ

Mouthwatering Models

Making a model of the problem-solving process gives students a good taste of two-digit by one-digit multiplication. In advance, use numbers less than 20 to write two-digit by one-digit multiplication problems on a student supply of nine-inch squares of pink construction paper. After reviewing the problem-solving process with students, give each child a prepared paper and a sheet of one-centimeter grid paper. A child cuts her grid paper to make an array of tens and ones that represents her assigned problem. She glues the array below the problem and labels it. Then she describes the rest of the problem-solving process as shown.

To make a strawberry-flavored ice-cream sandwich, staple the students' work between two nine-inch squares of brown construction paper. Write the title "Mouthwatering Multiplication" on the front cover and add desired decorations. Now, that's a booklet students will gladly sink their teeth into!

Sprinkles, Please!

This appetizing activity gives students another tasty experience with arrays! Using tagboard templates, each child traces a cone shape onto a 4" x 9" strip of brown construction paper and a scoop shape onto a nine-inch square of white construction paper. On the cone, he writes a two-digit by one-digit multiplication problem that has a two-digit factor of 19 or less. On the scoop, he draws and labels a colorful array of tens and ones that represents the problem (see the illustration). He cuts out both shapes. On the back of each one he writes the answer and his initials. Then he prepares two more problems in a like manner.

Later, have each child trade the six cutouts he prepared with a classmate. A student matches each array to its corresponding cone, copies and answers the problems on his math paper, and flips the cutouts to check his work. Then he trades the cutouts for a different set and repeats the activity. He continues in this manner until time is called. Ask each child to return his set of cutouts to its original owner, or collect the cutouts and place them at a center for more practice. Sprinkles, anyone?

Garret's
Multiplication
Sundae

Super-Duper Sundaes

Here's a quick-and-easy way to dish up two weeks' worth of challenging multiplication practice! Give each student a 9" x 12" white construction paper booklet that holds ten blank pages. Ask each child to draw the outline of an ice-cream dish on the front cover of his practice booklet and label the dish "[student name]'s Multiplication Sundae."

On each of the next ten school days, write a set of multiplication problems on the board for every child to copy and solve on a blank page in his booklet. Each day, assist students in checking their calculations. After any necessary corrections have been made, a student draws a star at the top of his booklet page and then colors an ice-cream scoop on the front cover of his booklet. When the child finishes the ten-day project, he adds desired decorations, such as whipping cream, nuts, and a cherry, to the super-duper sundae he has made. Multiplication practice is so delicious!

Scoop by Scoop

Multiplication enthusiasts stack up place-value and multiplication skills during this partner game! To make her game sheet, a student folds a sheet of blank paper in half lengthwise, unfolds the paper, and illustrates an ice-cream cone in the bottom left-hand corner. To the right of the fold line, she draws and numbers a framework for each of six two-digit by one-digit multiplication problems. When every child has prepared a game sheet, pair the students and give each twosome a die. Explain that one game consists of six rounds and that the object of each round is to have the larger product.

For each round of play, the partners take turns rolling the die. Each partner immediately records the number she rolls in the framework for that round. After the sixth roll, each partner solves the problem she's made. Next, the partners check each other's calculations. If both products are correct, the partner with the greater product draws and colors an ice-cream scoop on her cone. If only one product is correct, this partner adds a scoop to her cone. If neither product is correct, no scoops are awarded. The player with more scoops at the end of the sixth round wins!

How Many Scoops?

For additional servings of multiplying tens and ones, make a class set and a few extra copies of page 28. Have each child complete a copy of the page. Every few days, reprogram an unused copy of the page for another serving of frosty fun. To do this, white-out and then reprogram the quantity of treats on each order. Make student copies of the reprogrammed page, plus one extra. Program the extra copy for use as an answer key. Students are sure to agree that multiplying tens and ones is absolutely "ribbit-ing"!

Name____________________

A Super Scooper!

Find out how many ice-cream scoops must be made for each order.
Use the scoop chart.
Multiply.

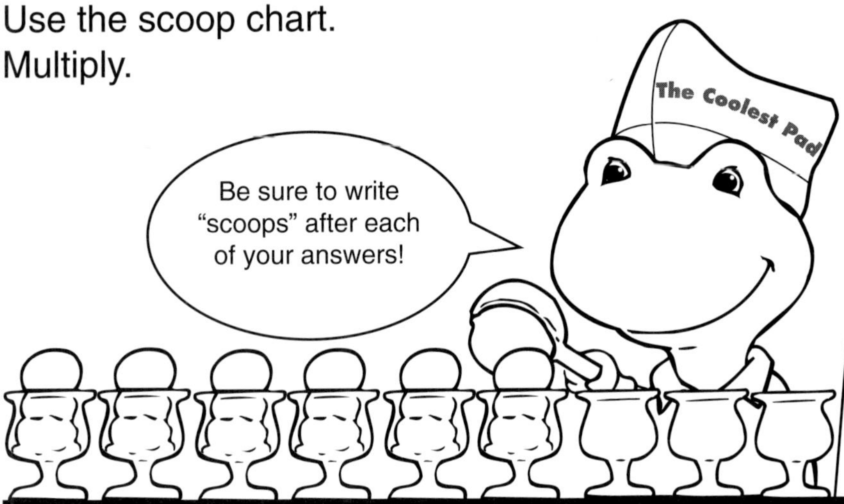
The Coolest Pad
Be sure to write "scoops" after each of your answers!

Scoop Chart

Double Dip..........2 scoops
Triple Treat ....3 scoops
King-Size Cup.....4 scoops
Super Sundae.....5 scoops
Colossal Cone ....6 scoops
Lily Pad Platter ...7 scoops

Order 1 12 King-Size Cups	**Order 2** 15 Triple Treats	**Order 3** 13 Colossal Cones	**Order 4** 18 Super Sundaes
Order 5 17 Lily Pad Platters	**Order 6** 19 Double Dips	**Order 7** 11 Triple Treats	**Order 8** 10 Colossal Cones
Order 9 16 Super Sundaes	**Order 10** 14 Double Dips	**Order 11** 12 Lily Pad Platters	**Order 12** 17 King-Size Cups

 Note to the teacher: Use this page with "How Many Scoops?" on page 27 .

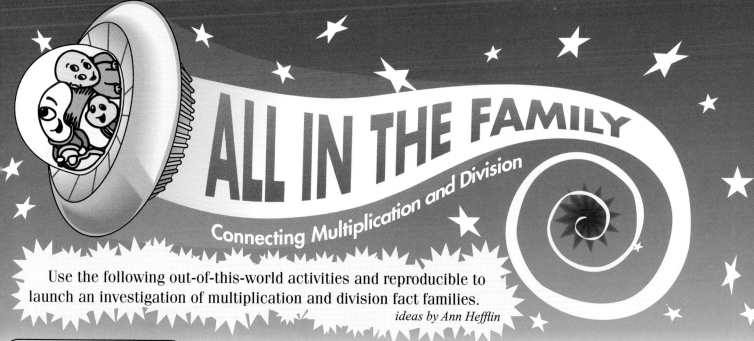

ALL IN THE FAMILY

Connecting Multiplication and Division

Use the following out-of-this-world activities and reproducible to launch an investigation of multiplication and division fact families.

ideas by Ann Hefflin

A Family Mission

During this hands-on activity, the relationship between multiplication and division takes shape! Pair students and give each pair a math mat and 15 counting cubes. Ask each pair to arrange its cubes in a three-row array. Help students understand that this array illustrates the multiplication fact shown as 3 x 5 = 15, and write the fact on the board. Then have each pair divide its cubes into three equal groups. Lead students to conclude that they have demonstrated the division fact 15 ÷ 3 = 5. Write this fact on the board too. Next, have each duo arrange its cubes in a five-row array (5 x 3 = 15) and then divide its cubes into five equal groups (15 ÷ 5 = 3). Write the corresponding facts on the board.

Ask students to describe how the four facts on the board are alike. Help them conclude that the same numbers appear in each one. Explain that a set of multiplication and division facts that uses the same numbers is called a *fact family*. As a class, discuss why a knowledge of fact families makes learning multiplication and division facts easier.

Continue your investigation by having the student pairs repeat the steps described with a smaller set of cubes. Then store a container of cubes in a math center for additional fact family exploration.

In a Spin!

Propel students' fact family knowledge to extraordinary heights with student-made spinners! To make a spinner, have each child divide a five-inch tagboard circle into eighths and randomly number the sections from 2 through 9. Then give each student a sheet of blank paper, a paper clip, and four small sticky notes. Ask each youngster to divide his blank paper into fourths. Next, have him use his pencil and paper clip to spin two numbers on his spinner. The student writes the two numbers and their product on a sticky note. He sticks the note onto his paper in the center of a box. Then, in each corner of the box, he writes a different fact from the corresponding fact family.

To continue, the child spins two more numbers and writes the numbers and their product on a blank sticky note. This time, he trades his note with a classmate. He sticks the note he receives on his paper in the center of a blank box and writes one fact in each corner as he has done before. He completes the remaining two boxes in a similar manner. Now, that's putting a fun spin on fact families!

Barry Slate

WE ARE FAMILY...

Far-Out Family Fun

There's plenty of fact family practice in a deck of multiplication flash cards! With students seated at their desks, determine an order of play. Begin play by showing the class a flash card. The first player stands, reads the problem, and answers it. The second player stands and states a different math fact that includes the same three numbers. The third and fourth players do likewise. Next, the four standing players clap their hands one time and say, "We are family!" The remainder of the class responds with a clap of hands and says, "They are family!" Then the first four players sit down. Show the class a different flash card and continue play along the predetermined route until each student has participated one or more times. Far out!

adapted from an idea by
Deborah Malicky
Rayne Elementary School
Clymer, PA

3...2...1...

Tricornered cards keep students in touch with fact families long after liftoff! Give each child six four-inch construction paper squares and a resealable plastic bag for card storage. Also list 12 products on the board.

A student cuts each square on the diagonal, creating 12 tricornered cards. To program a card, he writes a product from the board in the top corner and circles it. He writes two factors for the product in the two remaining corners. Next, he flips the card over and writes the corresponding fact family on the back. He programs one card for each product on the board. Then he stores the cards in his plastic bag.

To use his cards, a child removes one card from his bag, reads the three numbers on the front, states the corresponding fact family, and flips the card to verify his answers. Or he covers one corner of the card as he removes it from the bag. Then he determines the missing number, states the fact family, and verifies his answers. For a partner review, one student reads the three numbers on the front of the card (or two of them) and his partner provides the corresponding fact family (and missing number when appropriate).

$5 \times 9 = 45$
$9 \times 5 = 45$
$45 \div 9 = 5$
$45 \div 5 = 9$

45

5

9

Fact Family Blastoff!

Send students into orbit with fact family reinforcement! Give each child a copy of page 31 and two sheets of blank paper. Provide a stapler for student use. After each child locates and lists the hidden number sets, she completes the fact family assignment described in the Bonus Box. Mission accomplished!

Name _____

Fact Family Blastoff!

Find number sets that can be used to make fact families.
List 8 different sets below each spacecraft.
You will use each number one or more times.

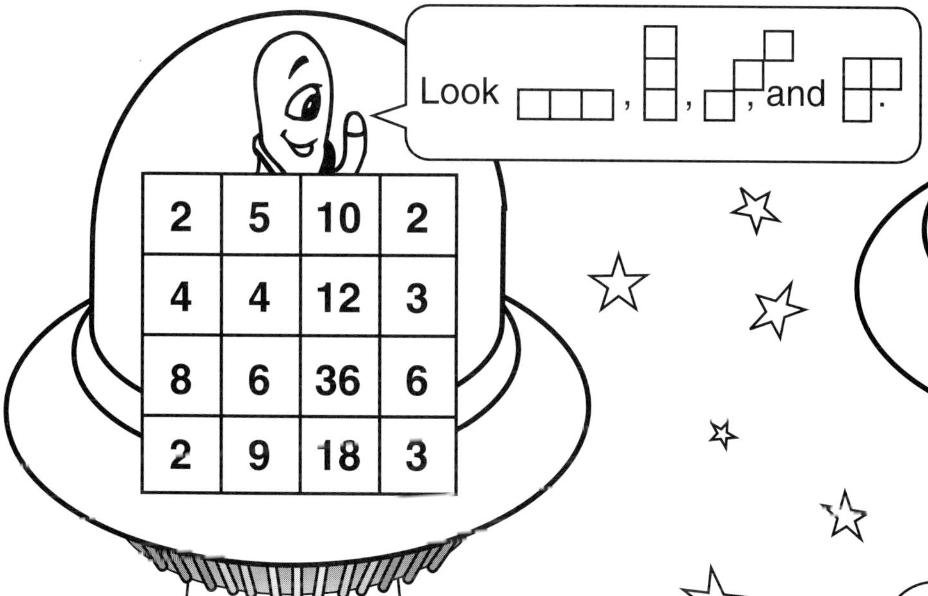

Look ⬚⬚⬚ , ⬚ , ⬚ , and ⬚ .

2	5	10	2
4	4	12	3
8	6	36	6
2	9	18	3

45	9	20	10
5	4	2	5
8	36	10	30
4	2	3	6

Cosmic Force

_____ , _____ , _____

_____ , _____ , _____

_____ , _____ , _____

_____ , _____ , _____

_____ , _____ , _____

_____ , _____ , _____

_____ , _____ , _____

_____ , _____ , _____

Star Cruiser

_____ , _____ , _____

_____ , _____ , _____

_____ , _____ , _____

_____ , _____ , _____

_____ , _____ , _____

_____ , _____ , _____

_____ , _____ , _____

_____ , _____ , _____

Bonus Box: Title one sheet of blank paper with the name of each spacecraft. On each paper write the fact family for each number set found on the spacecraft. When you finish, staple the two papers to this paper.

Note to the teacher: Use with "Fact Family Blastoff!" on page 30.

Knights of the Rounding Table

Step back into medieval days to strengthen students' skills in rounding numbers. Your young pages will soon be rounding numbers with royal success!

A Royal Tip

Remembering when to round to the greater ten becomes perfectly clear with a visual image! Ask each child to picture himself boarding a medieval-themed roller coaster at point zero. As his dragon-shaped car slowly inches up a steep hill, he chugs past the numbers one, two, three, and four. But when he reaches number five at the tippy top of the hill, his car suddenly zooms down the other side of the hill and stops at the number ten! With this visual image in mind, students are sure to remember that the number five means zoom ahead to the next ten!

Elizabeth Roberts—Gr. 2, Manor Elementary School, Levittown, PA

Conquer the Castle!

This partner game is packed with opportunities to round numbers to the nearest ten. To make his game, a child colors a copy of page 33. Next, he cuts along the dotted line, sets the castle gameboard aside, and cuts out the game pieces. Provide a quart-size resealable plastic bag for game storage.

Pair students and have each player stack his game pieces facedown. Explain that the object of the game is for a player to be first to reach the top of his castle. Each player begins play at the ground level of his castle. To take a turn, both players simultaneously draw their top game pieces. Each player rounds the number on his game piece to the nearest ten. If this number appears on the ground level of his castle, he covers it with his game piece. If not, he places the piece in a personal discard pile (which is later shuffled and reused). After both players play their game pieces, the two players take another turn by together drawing their top game pieces. When a player covers two spaces on the ground level of his castle, his play proceeds to the next castle level. Play continues in this manner until one player covers two spaces at each level of his castle and then covers the winning space at the top of his castle. Now, that's a game that's sure to be played again and again!

Janet Ranieri—Gr. 3, Lowell Elementary, Rock Springs, WY

The Rounding Table

Here's a manipulative that gives students a leg up on rounding to the nearest hundred! Give each child a copy of "The Rounding Table" from page 34 and a business-size envelope (for storage). Have each child color the artwork and cut along the dotted lines.

To use his table, a child determines the two hundreds between which the number he is rounding falls and places the matching cutout in the provided spaces. If the number he is rounding has less than five tens, he rounds to the lesser hundred. If it has five tens or more, he rounds to the greater hundred. After a bit of practice, dub your students knights of the rounding table and have them complete "Nifty Number Shields" from page 34.

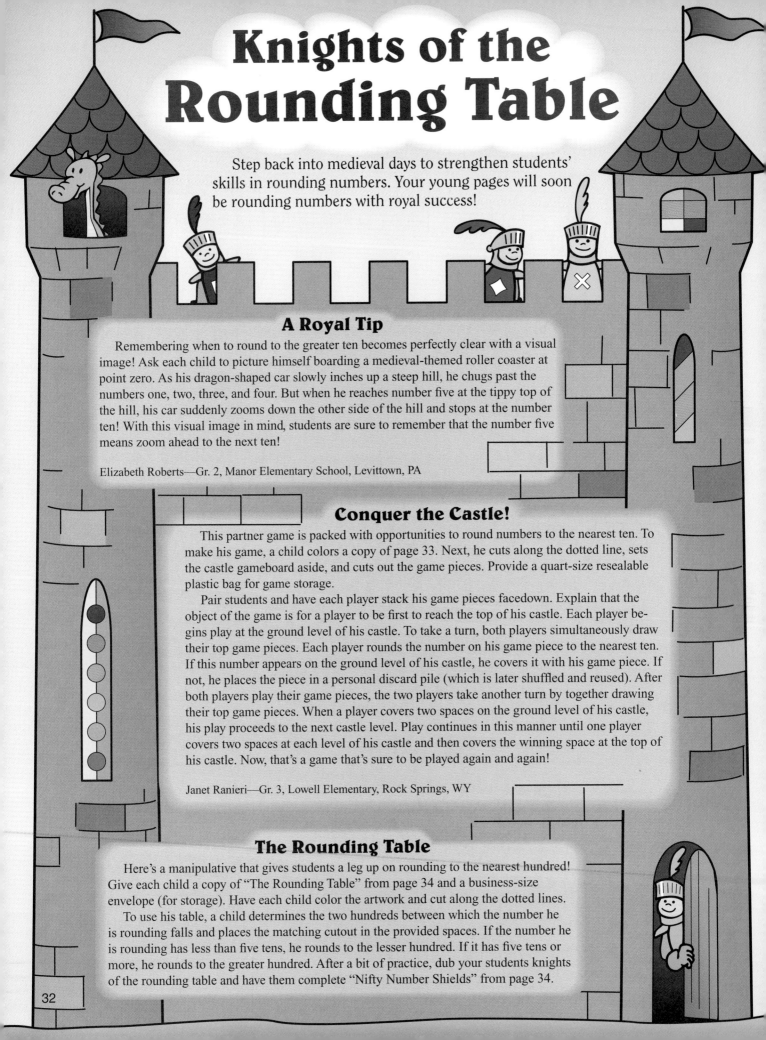

Game Pieces

5	75	18	3	61
24	93	87	77	25
22	59	13	65	84
41	44	27	1	52
48	31	82	7	67
88	17	4	73	47
39	55	94	14	35

Conquer the Castle!

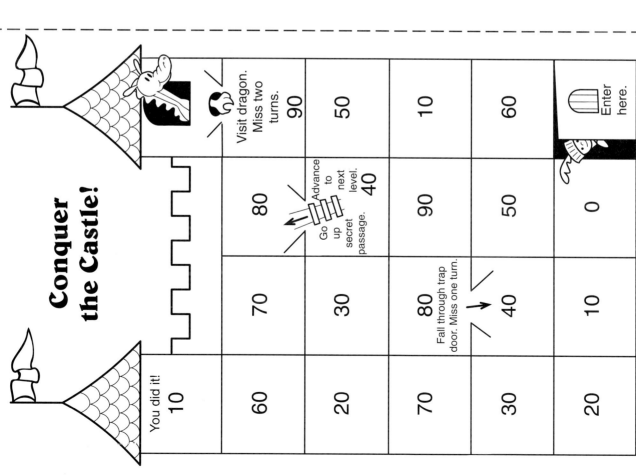

Note to the teacher: Use with "Conquer the Castle!" on page 32.

Nifty Number Shields

Round each number to the nearest hundred.
Write your answer on the line.
Use the code to color each shield.

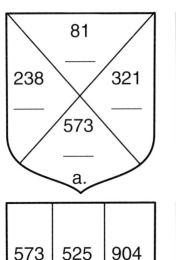

a.
81
238   321
573

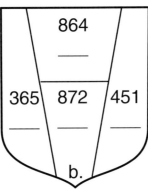

b.
864
365 872 451

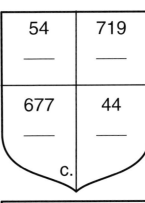

c.
54   719
677   44

d.
573 525 904

e.
832
29
442

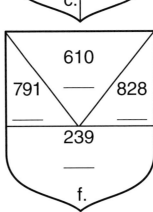

f.
610
791   828
239

Color Code
0, 100   = blue
200, 300 = green
400, 500 = yellow
600, 700 = red
800, 900 = purple

Bonus Box: How is rounding to the nearest hundred like rounding to the nearest ten? Write your answer on the back of this paper.

The Rounding Table

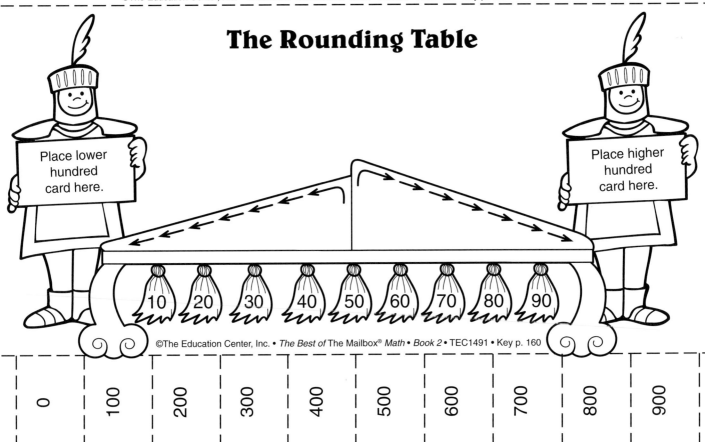

Place lower hundred card here.

Place higher hundred card here.

10 20 30 40 50 60 70 80 90

0   100   200   300   400   500   600   700   800   900

Note to the teacher: Use "Nifty Number Shields" and "The Rounding Table" with "The Rounding Table" on page 32.

Now Serving:
Fractions!

DELICIOUS!

WHOLESOME!

Served fresh daily!

After sampling these appetizing math activities, students are sure to agree that fractions are as easy as pie!

Take Part

Any way you slice it, this hands-on fraction activity is guaranteed to please! Have each student work on waxed paper to shape a small portion of play dough into a square. Next, have him use a plastic knife to cut the square into two equal-size parts, pointing out that there is more than one way to do this. Invite several students to the chalkboard to draw how they divided their squares. Add to these illustrations as needed to provide a variety of solutions. Then choose a halved square and explain that each part of the square is one-half of its shape. Demonstrate how to write "1/2" and ask each child to use a toothpick to write the fraction on each half of his square. Then have him smooth and reshape his dough to explore thirds and fourths in a similar manner. Now, that's an idea that's a cut above the rest!

Carol Newland—Gr. 2, Banner County School, Harrisburg, NE

Pie Problems

When two friends have one scrumptious pie, what do they do? They share it equally, of course! Give each student two identical white circles, a 12" x 18" sheet of white construction paper, and a card labeled with a group of animals like "5 squirrels" or "8 giraffes." A student colors one circle to resemble a pie the animals might enjoy; then she colors the second circle to match. Next, she glues one pie on the left half of her paper. She cuts the other pie into equal-size pieces for the animals and glues the pieces on the right half of her paper. Then she labels her paper in a manner similar to what is shown. Students quickly see that equal shares are only fair!

A banana pie for eight monkeys.

Each monkey gets 1/8 of the pie.

Sorting Fractions

The fraction cards on page 39 provide students with all sorts of practice identifying parts of a figure!

- **For an individual activity,** give each child a 12" x 18" sheet of construction paper and a copy of page 39. A student folds the construction paper in half twice and then unfolds it to reveal four boxes. She cuts out the four labels from her copy of page 39 and glues each one in a different box. Then she cuts out the fraction cards, sorts them into the labeled boxes, and glues them in place. Challenge students to write a fraction for each card in the "Other" box.

- **For a center activity,** laminate a construction paper copy of page 39 and cut along the bold lines. Use a permanent marker to code the backs of the cards for self-checking. Store the cutouts in a zippered bag and place the bag at a math center. A student sorts the cards into the four designated groups and then flips them to check his work.

35

Spill the Beans

At this center, spills create fractions—not messes! Spray-paint one side of a supply of dried kidney beans. When the paint is dry, place varying numbers of the beans in several empty film containers. Store the containers in a shoebox at the center. Also provide crayons and a supply of paper. A child removes the lid from the shoebox, chooses a container, and carefully spills the beans from it into the lid. She illustrates the spilled beans on her paper and writes a fraction for each set of sprayed and unsprayed beans shown. Then she returns the beans to the container and repeats the process with the remaining containers. To increase the difficulty of the center, use two different colors of spray paint to paint the beans.

Cindy Wann—Gr. 3
Westside Elementary
Jonesboro, AR

$\frac{7}{10}$ brown $\frac{3}{10}$ orange

Fraction "Stamp-ede"

Count on students to give this partner activity their stamp of approval! Have each student fold a large sheet of drawing paper in half three times and then unfold his paper to reveal eight equal-size sections. After he traces the fold lines, he uses a stamper to make several images in each section. Then he circles a desired number of images in each group. Next, he trades papers with a classmate. In each section of his classmate's paper, he writes what fraction of the stamps in that group are circled. When he finishes, he returns the paper to his partner for verification, and he verifies the activity he created and his partner completed.

If you have a computer and a program that has stamp tools such as Kid Pix Studio or Fine Artist, have students prepare (and complete) computer-generated activities.

Nancy Hyrczyk—Grs. 1–2
Eisenhower School
Prospect Heights, IL

Family-Style Fractions

Fraction skills are all in the family with this nifty idea! To begin, ask a few boys and girls to stand at the front of the room. With input from the rest of the class, identify the fraction that names the male part of the group and the fraction that names the female part of the group. Write these fractions on the chalkboard. Repeat the process with several different groups of students. Then explore fractional parts of a different type of group—the family. To do this, each child chooses an attribute such as hair or eye color by which to describe herself and her family members. On provided paper, she draws her family in two or more sets by the chosen attribute. Then she labels each set with the corresponding fraction. Display students' completed work on a bulletin board titled "Fractions Are All in the Family!"

$\frac{2}{5}$ of my family has blonde hair $\frac{3}{5}$ of my family has brown hair

I have $\frac{1}{2}$ dozen eggs.

Fabulous Fraction Diary

A fraction a day builds skills in a fun way! Have each student staple four sheets of blank paper inside construction paper covers. Ask her to label the front cover "Fraction Diary" and personalize it as desired. Then have her label one blank page for each day of the week. Every day the student describes and illustrates at least one fraction she encounters (at home, at school, or in the community). After seven days, invite each student to share her favorite or most unique entry with the class.

adapted from an idea by
MaryMargaret Clement
Cohoes, NY

Real-World Fractions

$\frac{1}{3}$	:	1 wheel of a tricycle
$\frac{1}{8}$	:	1 stick of gum from a package
$\frac{1}{12}$	:	1 month of the year
$\frac{2}{12}$	:	2 eggs from a dozen
$\frac{3}{4}$	:	3 sections of a cracker
$\frac{2}{6}$	:	

On the Lookout

This activity reminds students that fractions aren't just in math class—they're everywhere! Show a few examples of real-world fractions, such as an orange cut into quarters or one-half of a pair of shoes. Then ask students to brainstorm additional examples, and list their ideas on chart paper. Next, give each student a large index card bearing a fraction. For homework have him find an example of the fraction at home and then illustrate it on the back of the card. Or invite students to bring examples of their assigned fractions to school on a predetermined date. With this engaging approach to math, your youngsters will be keeping their eyes peeled for fractions for a long time to come!

Leigh Anne Newsom—Gr. 3
Greenbrier Intermediate School
Chesapeake, VA

Fraction Diary

My dad made pancakes this morning. He used $1\frac{1}{4}$ cups of flour and $\frac{1}{2}$ teaspoon of salt.

For Good Measure

Fractions really measure up with this tasty classroom recipe! On a copy of page 40, list three snack mix ingredients in the "Ingredient List" box at the bottom of the page. (The third ingredient will make up most of the recipe.) Then distribute a class supply of the page. Explain to students that they will be writing a recipe for snack mix. Guide students through the activity, providing assistance as needed. When the recipe is written, ask each child to bring one-quarter cup of a designated ingredient to school the following day. Use the class-created recipe to make a batch of snack mix for your students' eating pleasure. Periodically repeat the activity, varying the ingredients used and the number of people eating the snack mix. Students quickly discover that fractions are not only handy, but downright delicious!

Dolores Joiner—Gr. 1
Furry Elementary
Sandusky, OH

37

In a Word

What's in a word? Plenty of fraction practice! Prepare a form like the one shown and give each student a copy. Dictate six words and ask each student to write each one on the appropriate line. Then instruct the youngster to write one fraction for the part of the word that is vowels and one for the part that is consonants. After each child has completed her work, describe each dictated word by announcing its corresponding fractions. Challenge students to identify the word you have described. To extend older students' learning, ask them what they notice about the *numerators* and *denominators* for each word's fractions. Lead them to conclude that the sum of the numerators equals the denominator.

Melanie J. Miller
Nashport, OH

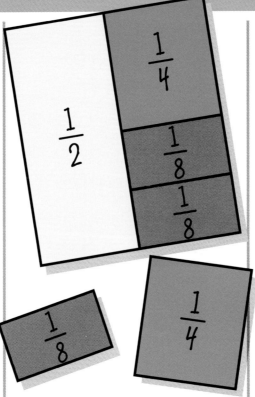

Colorful Equivalents

The concept of equivalent fractions takes shape with these student-made manipulatives! Give each student four nine-inch construction paper squares, each a different color. To prepare a set of manipulatives, a student writes "1" on one square to represent a whole. He folds another square in half, opens it, cuts along the fold line to make two equal parts, and labels each resulting half "1/2." He uses a similar process with the two remaining squares to make and label four quarters and eight eighths. Then ask each student to determine different ways to completely cover the whole square with assorted manipulatives without overlapping any pieces. Invite students to share their solutions.

For more exploration with equivalents, have each youngster use his manipulatives to determine how many eighths are needed to cover one-fourth and how many fourths are needed to cover one-half. To reuse the manipulatives, have each child store his set in a large resealable zippered bag.

adapted from an idea by
Phil Forsythe—Gr. 3
Northeastern Elementary
Bellefontaine, OH

A Menu of Fraction Books

If your students are hungry to learn more about fractions, whet their appetites with these terrific titles!

Fraction Fun
Written by David A. Adler
Illustrated by Nancy Tobin

Jump, Kangaroo, Jump!
Written by Stuart J. Murphy
Illustrated by Kevin O'Malley

Fraction Action
By Loreen Leedy

Give Me Half!
Written by Stuart J. Murphy
Illustrated by G. Brian Karas

$\dfrac{1}{2}$	$\dfrac{1}{3}$	$\dfrac{1}{4}$	other

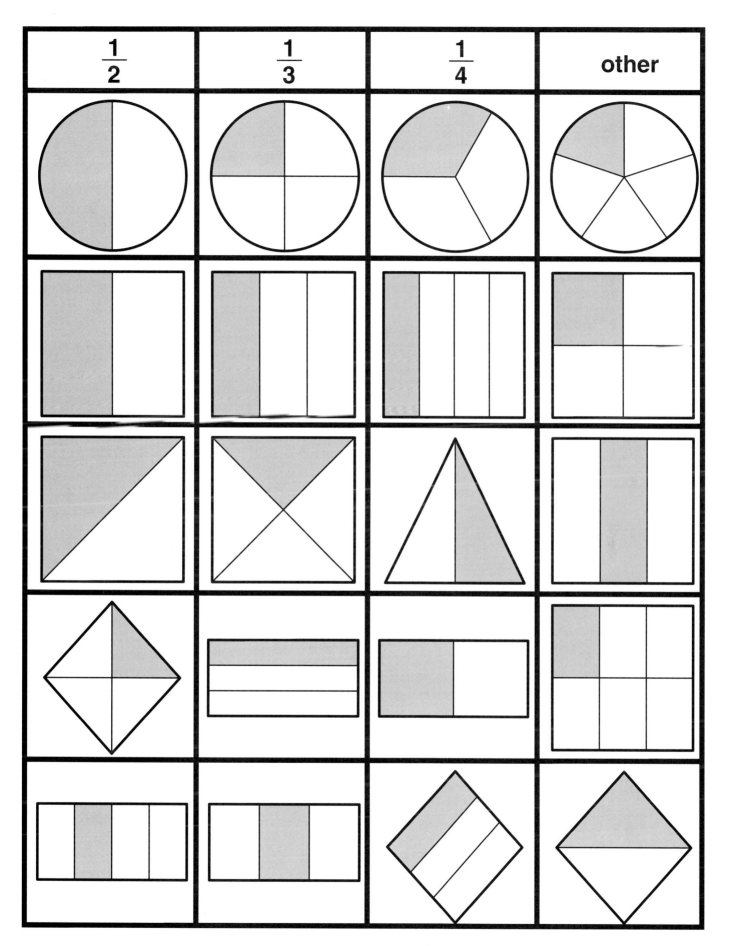

©The Education Center, Inc. • *The Best of* The Mailbox® *Math* • *Book 2* • TEC1491

Note to the teacher: Use with "Sorting Fractions" on page 35.

39

Super Snack Mix

Write a snack mix recipe!

1. How many people will eat snack mix? _____

2. Color $\frac{1}{4}$ of a measuring cup for each person who is eating snack mix. Start with the first cup.

3. Study the measuring cups.
   How much snack mix do you need? _____

4. Write an ingredient below each cup you colored. Use the ingredient list.

5. Finish the recipe below.

A. _____ **B.** _____ **C.** _____ **C.** _____ **C.** _____

C. _____ **C.** _____ **C.** _____ **C.** _____ **C.** _____

Super Snack Mix
(Serves _____ people)

_____ of ingredient **A.**

_____ of ingredient **B.**

_____ of ingredient **C.**

Mix well. Serve each person $\frac{1}{4}$ cup.

Ingredient List

A. _____

B. _____

C. _____

Note to the teacher: Use with "For Good Measure" on page 37.

The Numeral Cafe

Scrambled Eggs?

Your youngsters will absolutely love this math-review game—and you will too! Cut out one construction paper egg for each student plus five more for good measure. Sequentially number the eggs and write a different math problem on each one. Solve each problem on the other side of the egg as shown. Tape one egg—the top only—to each child's desk so that the unsolved problem is showing. Tape the additional eggs to five extra student desks (with chairs) or to a reading table with five chairs.

To play this game, each child personalizes a sheet of paper. On your signal of "Ready," each child stands up and pushes in her chair. On your signal of "Scramble," each child takes her paper and pencil to another desk, copies the problem and its number on her paper, and solves the problem. On your signal of "Check," each student flips the egg and checks her work. Continue play in this manner until students have completed a desired number of problems. Then have students return to their desks. They will have had a great time practicing their math skills, and you won't be faced with a stack of math papers to correct! Now, that's a Grade-A math game!

Jeannie Hinyard—Gr. 2, Welder Elementary, Sinton, TX

A Calculated Guess

Sharpen your students' mental-math skills with this quick-and-easy small- or large-group game. Give each child a laminated card labeled either "Add [numeral]" or "Subtract [numeral]." On the chalkboard write a game numeral that is greater than the greatest numeral shown on a "subtract" card. Select one student to start. This student follows the direction on his card and announces the new game numeral. For example, if the game numeral on the board is 15 and the student's card reads "Add 3," he announces the new numeral 18. The first classmate who, when called upon, correctly identifies the math calculation (*add 3*) takes his turn next. This student then applies his card's direction to the most recent game numeral (*in this case it is 18*). Play continues in this manner until each child has taken at least one turn or game time is over.

Miriane Krauss—Gr. 3, Bais Yaakov of Brooklyn, Brooklyn, NY

Add, Subtract, or Multiply

Here's a partner game that's versatile, practical, and fun for kids. What more could you need? To make a gameboard, program a tic-tac-toe grid with nine numerals; then make a copy for every two students. Pair the children and distribute the gameboards. Each student also needs a blank sheet of paper and a pencil.

To play, announce a math operation: *addition, subtraction, or multiplication.* Then, on your signal, each student refers to the gameboard to create and solve as many math problems as she can. To create an acceptable math problem, the two numbers used must be in boxes that touch horizontally, vertically, or diagonally. When time is called, each student compares her work with her partner's. To earn a point, a student must have created and solved a problem that her partner did not. The partner with the most points wins the game.

adapted from an idea by Debbie M. Darling—Gr. 3
Dolphin Terrace Elementary, El Paso, TX

Roll It!

Mental-math skills are put to the test with this large-group game. In an open area, have students sit on the floor, forming a circle. Announce a number range (like 0–9) and a math operation (addition, subtraction, or multiplication). Give one student a small rubber ball. To begin play, this student declares a number as he rolls the ball to another classmate. This classmate declares a number as he rolls the ball to a third classmate. The third classmate uses the two called numerals and the stated math operation to form an equation. If the student is correct, he begins the next round of play. If he is incorrect, he rolls the ball to a fourth classmate, who attempts to provide a correct equation. When a correct answer is given, play resumes as described above. If desired, ask students who answered incorrectly to sit out the next round of play. Continue play until each student has participated at least once. As students become familiar with the game, encourage them to increase its pace. That's when the fun really begins!

Sheila Jessup—Gr. 1, Button Gwinnett Elementary, Hinesville, GA

Tic-Tac-Toe Math

Play this large- or small-group math game in an instant! To make the gameboard, each student draws a tic-tac-toe grid on a piece of paper and writes a different numeral in each game space. Limit students' numeral choices. For example, to review basic addition facts, ask students to use the numerals 0–18 (for basic subtraction facts: 0–9; for basic multiplication facts: 0–50). In turn, each child announces a math fact that equals an answer on her gameboard. Every student who has that answer on her gameboard crosses it off. Keep a running list of each math fact given. The first student to cross off three sums (differences, products) in a vertical, horizontal, or diagonal row declares, "Tic-tac-toe!" She then calls out the three answers she has crossed out for your verification. Once a winner of the game has been confirmed, each student quickly draws another gameboard, and play begins again.

Marilyn Webb—Gr. 1, Brookhouse School, Dartmouth,
Nova Scotia, Canada

Pam Crane

The Math Pattern Express
A Trainload of Math-Related Patterning Experiences

With this precious pattern cargo, it's full steam ahead for miles and miles of mathematical learning. All aboard!

Engineers in Training

Warm up your youngsters' patterning skills with a verbal response activity. On the board list words that describe train noises, such as *choo, toot, chug,* and *woo.* Then select words from the list and use them to create a simple verbal pattern like *choo, choo, toot.* Repeat the pattern several times, inviting students to join in when they recognize the pattern. Practice a variety of verbal patterns in this way. When your young engineers are on track, challenge them to add body motions to the patterns! *Choo, woo, chug, chug, chug...*

Individual Trains

Every engineer needs a train! In fact, several of the activities in this collection can't be completed without one! Give each child a white construction paper copy of page 45 and a resealable plastic bag. To make his train, a student personalizes and colors the train engine, uses the code to color the symbols on the boxcars, and cuts out the patterns on the bold lines. Then he stores his cutouts inside the resealable plastic bag for later use.

Unloading Nonpatterns

At this train station, blowing the whistle on nonpatterned loads is just part of an engineer's job! Have each child place her train cutouts from "Individual Trains" atop her desk. Then specify a color (or symbol) and instruct each student to connect a matching boxcar to her engine. Continue in this manner until four boxcars are added. Ask students to examine the resulting load and then give a thumbs-up for a patterned load or a thumbs-down for a nonpatterned load. After a volunteer explains why the load is patterned or nonpatterned, have students unload the boxcars and prepare for a new load. Continue in this manner for as long as desired, adjusting the number of boxcars per load and the complexity of each pattern or nonpattern to match your students' capabilities.

43

Picking Up Patterns

It's full steam ahead when students pair up to make and extend patterns! First have each child initial the backs of his cutouts from "Individual Trains." Then pair students. Partner 1 connects two boxcars to his engine cutout. Partner 2 repeats the established pattern by adding two of his own boxcars to the load. The partners, in turn, continue extending the pattern until their supply of appropriate cars runs out. Together the partners confirm that the pattern is complete and then each partner retrieves his boxcars. Partner 2 begins a new patterning activity by connecting two boxcars to his engine. Have student pairs continue making and extending patterns for as long as desired. To increase the challenge, instruct student pairs to extend each initial pattern to three or four boxcars.

Undercover Cargo

Identifying the pattern is the key to cracking the case of the undercover cargo! Using her cutouts from "Individual Trains," have each child form the following train: engine, red car, green car, triangle car, square car, circle car, blue car, square car, green car. Challenge each child to identify the train's pattern *(red, green, blue* or *square, circle, triangle)* and group the boxcars accordingly. If students are having difficulty, suggest that they look to find where the pattern begins repeating. Present several more cargo challenges—varying between two-, three-, four-, and five-car repeating cargo patterns. When you wrap up, invite students to pair up with a partner during free time and use their cutouts to create additional concealed cargo patterns!

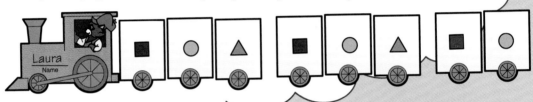

Boxcar Confusion

Patterning skills come in handy at a mixed-up train yard! To prove your point, have each child use his engine and boxcar cutouts (from "Individual Trains") to form the following train: engine, red car, blue car, green car, red car, blue car, green car, green car, blue car, red car. Explain that because two boxcars on the train have been accidentally switched, this train has lost its pattern. Suggest that students find the switched boxcars by first identifying the train's repeating pattern. When the switched boxcars are found, give students another boxcar mystery to solve.

For additional practice, have each child use his cutouts to make a train with a repeating pattern and then switch two boxcars on his train. Pair students and have each child solve his partner's boxcar mystery. Use "Cargo Switcheroo!" on page 46 to further reinforce your students' patterning skills.

Staying on Track

Daily practice is the ticket to keeping your engineers' patterning skills on track! For easy management, have each child record his patterning practice in an engineer's log. Give each child a copy of the engine pattern on page 45 to personalize and color. Then have him cut out the pattern and glue it onto the front cover of a booklet of blank pages. Each day provide a pattern with a corresponding task for students to complete in their logs. Choo, choo!

2, 2, 4, 3, 3, 6, 4, 4, 8

Name

Color code: △ = blue □ = red ○ = green

Name ____________________

Cargo Switcheroo!

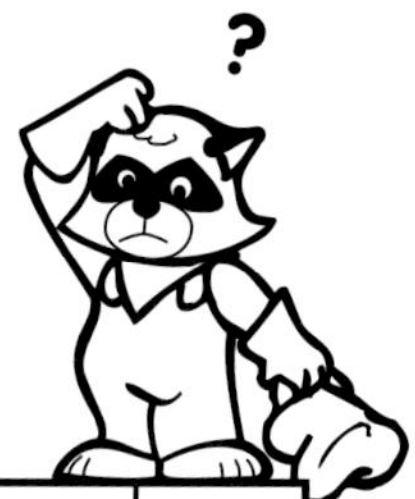

On each track two pieces of cargo are switched.
Find the repeating pattern and then circle the switched cargo.
Cut out the new cargo below and glue it in place.

△	○	△	○	△	△	△	○	△	○	○	○

□	X	X	□	X	□	□	X	X	X	X	X

A	C	Z	A	C	Z	A	Z	C	A	C	Z

6	6	5	5	6	5	5	6	5	5	5	5

Train Cargo				
	○	×	Z	5
	◁	□	C	6

Bonus Box: Color the cargo on each track without changing its pattern.

 Note to the teacher: Use with "Boxcar Confusion" on page 44.

A JUNGLE OF GEOMETRY

If you'd like to know how other teachers across the country reinforce geometry concepts, take a trek through this jungle. Nestled among the foliage you'll find ideas for strengthening a menagerie of skills, from recognizing flat shapes to understanding symmetry. It's just what you need to get your youngsters into the swing of geometry!

BACKGROUND FOR THE TEACHER

In this collection of ideas, the term *flat shape* will describe a two-dimensional shape (also called a *plane figure*), such as a circle or a square. The term *solid shape* will describe any three-dimensional shape (also called a *space figure*), such as a sphere, cone, or cube.

SHAPELY JUNGLE

Do you wish your students were WILD about geometry? Try this! Create a simple jungle backdrop for a large bulletin board and add the title "Shapely Jungle." To introduce the activity, share with your students Lois Ehlert's *Color Farm* or *Color Zoo.* In each book, assorted flat shapes are used to create nine animals living in the named habitat. Have students recall the flat shapes used in the book and name additional ones. Then write a student-generated list of jungle animals. Next, challenge each child to create a jungle animal for the display by cutting out and gluing together assorted construction paper shapes. For best results, provide shape templates in a variety of sizes. Showcase the completed projects at the display.

Vickie Carter
Keller, TX

SHAPE DETECTIVES

Put your youngsters hot on the trail of flat shapes! Ask students to pretend that they are detectives who have been assigned to a very important case—tracking down missing flat shapes. Provide a list of shapes that are hiding throughout the classroom, such as circles, squares, triangles, and rectangles. Then have each supersleuth choose a shape from the list and write its name on a copy of page 53. To complete the activity, the student illustrates an animated likeness of the flat shape, carefully describes the shape, lists three or more places where it has been seen, and signs his name. Set aside time for students to share their completed work with their classmates. Now, that's a fun way to track down shapes!

Debbie Murphy, Goodnoe Elementary
Holland, PA

MISSING SHAPE

Name of shape: Sneaky Square

Description of shape: It has four lines that are all the same length. It has four corners. It is a closed shape

This shape has been seen posing as the cover of a book, a yellow sticky note, a section of the calendar, and a space on a gameboard.

Information provided by Detective Gregory Cap

Barry Slate

I would like to be a triangle. I would slip into the place where my teacher puts her hand on her hip. I would know _all_ the answers!

OH, THE PLACES POLYGONS GO!

Use this creative-thinking activity to get to the point of _polygons_—flat, closed shapes with three or more straight lines. Read aloud _The Greedy Triangle_ by Marilyn Burns. In this humorous tale, a triangle is unhappy with its shape and chooses time and again to add an extra line and angle to its figure. In the end, the greedy shape decides that three sides makes a perfect polygon! To find out which polygons your youngsters prefer, ask students to recall things the following polygons do in the story: triangle, quadrilateral, pentagon, hexagon. If desired, list their ideas on the chalkboard under the appropriate headings. Then have each student use a 9" x 12" sheet of drawing paper to illustrate the shape she would most like to be and write an explanation for her choice. Encourage each child to design a colorful border around her work that incorporates her chosen shape. Bind the completed projects into a class book titled "Polygons On Location!"

Amanda Dolan
Walpole, MA

KING-SIZE POLYGONS

Cooperation is the key to this shapely activity. For every three students, cut a four-yard length of yarn (or string) and securely tie the ends. Distribute the yarn rings and instruct each group to form a triangle with its yarn. Ask students how many sides (corners) the polygon has and whether all three sides of a triangle must be equal in length. Then reorganize the students so that each group of four has one yarn ring. Have each group use its yarn to form a rectangle and then a square. Pose questions that require the students to examine and compare the shapes they've formed. Continue reorganizing the groups to form pentagons, hexagons, octagons, and so on. Students will agree that this hands-on idea has king-size appeal!

Barbara Bunzol
Arlington Heights, IL

SIZING UP CONGRUENCY

This large-group game has students sizing up _congruent figures_ (figures of the same size and shape). For every two students, cut out two congruent construction paper shapes, making sure all cutouts are the same color. Laminate the shapes for durability; then hole-punch each shape, thread a length of yarn through the hole, and tie the yarn's ends. To play, randomly distribute the resulting shape necklaces. Each student places his necklace around his neck and searches for the classmate who has a congruent shape. To determine whether two shapes are congruent, the students stack their shapes one atop the other. If the shapes are congruent, the pair sits down. When everyone is sitting, collect the necklaces and play the game again!

SHAPE IT!

Get students in touch with solid shapes! Give each child a golf ball–size portion of modeling clay. Announce a solid shape—such as a sphere, cube, cone, box, or cylinder—and challenge students to form the shape with their clay. Verify each child's work; then repeat the activity for each solid shape being studied. This kinesthetic learning process is sure to give students a good feel for solid shapes.

Ruth Heller—Gr. 3
Public School 156
Laurelton, NY

This picture shows the flagpole at the front of our school. The flagpole is a cylinder.

THE GREAT SHAPE HUNT

Head outdoors for this solid shape hunt! You need a camera and film with enough exposures for every two students to take one photograph. Pair students and lead them around the school grounds. Ask each twosome to locate an object that represents a solid shape the class is studying. Assist each pair in photographing the object it identifies and make a note of what the pair photographs. When the pictures are developed, have each twosome make a page for a class book. To do this, a pair glues its photograph on a 6" x 9" sheet of construction paper. Then it describes the photographed shape on a large index card. In its description, the pair includes the name of the photographed object, where it is located, and the solid shape it represents. Then the pair glues its index card to the back of its mounted photograph. Compile these pages into a class book titled "Name That Shape." Place the book at a math center. To complete the center, a student studies each photograph, determines the solid shape it represents, and turns the page to check his answer.

Carrie Hursh—Gr. 1
Harrison Elementary
Harrison, OH

SNACKTIME SHAPE-UP

This solid shape review is a tasty experience! Give each student a resealable plastic bag containing snack items that are cubes, boxes, cylinders, spheres, and cones. Consider items like cheese cubes, caramel candies, stick pretzels, marshmallows, malted milk balls, Bugles corn snacks, and candy kisses. Then announce a solid shape and ask students to remove the corresponding snack items from their bags. Have the students examine the snack items to determine how many sides, corners, and edges (if any) the solid shape has; then invite the students to eat those snacks. Repeat the activity for each snack shape. Delicious!

Cindy Boger—Gr. 2, Balls Creek Elementary School, Newton, NC
Dianne Neumann—Gr. 2, Frank C. Whiteley School, Hoffman Estates, IL

IMPORTANT SHAPES

What's so important about solid shapes? Plenty! To prepare for this writing activity, write the name of each solid shape your students are studying on an individual length of bulletin board paper. Also display a sample of each shape. To review each shape, have the students pass around the sample and name the shape's unique qualities. List their ideas on the appropriate poster. Next, read aloud Margaret Wise Brown's *The Important Book*. Discuss the repetitive nature of the book's text and talk about how this pattern can be used to create pages for a class book titled "The Important Book of Solid Shapes." To make her page for the book, a student chooses a solid shape and describes important things about it. If desired, specify that each student page tell how many *faces, corners,* and *edges* the shape has and name three or more objects of that shape. After reading this class publication, students are sure to agree that solid shapes are very important!

Katherine Ritchie Dent—Gr. 2
Miami Country Day School
Miami, FL

The important thing about a
CUBE
is that all of its faces are the same size.

A cube looks like an ice cube or an alphabet block. A game die is a cube too.
A cube has 8 corners.
A cube has 6 faces.
A cube has 12 edges.
But
the important thing about a cube is that all of its faces are the same size.

GROCERY BAG GEOMETRY

Recognizing solid shapes is in the bag—the grocery bag, that is! For this small-group activity, you need one large paper grocery bag per group. For easy management, program each bag with a different number or letter; then, in each bag, place ten nonbreakable, everyday items that represent the solid shapes your students are studying. Be sure to vary the contents of each bag. To begin, have each group remove and study each item in its bag. Then, on your signal, have each group return the ten items to the bag. Next, challenge each group to recall each item it studied and write the name and shape of the item on a sheet of paper. When appropriate, have each group check its resulting list against the items in its bag. Then rotate the bags among the groups and repeat the activity. Continue in this manner until each group has completed the activity with every bag.

adapted from an idea by Shelly Lanier
Reeds Elementary
Lexington, NC

WELCOME TO SHAPESVILLE

Find out how well your youngsters' knowledge of shapes is shaping up with this hands-on activity. A week or two in advance, invite students to bring to school clean and empty boxes (cereal, gift, shoe), cardboard tubes, and other such items that represent solid shapes. Also provide an assortment of construction paper and shape templates. When there is an ample supply of materials, inform students that their next geometry assignment is to create a community called Shapesville from shapes! Ask students to brainstorm structures and locations to include in the community, and list their ideas on the chalkboard. Next, have each child select one or more items from the list to create. On a designated date, have each child present his completed project(s) to the class and identify several of the shapes he used. Then enlist your students' help in organizing the projects on a paper-covered table. For a fun follow-up, each day post the name of a solid or flat shape and challenge students to find as many examples of the shape as they can in Shapesville!

Sherra Sterling—Grs. 2–3
Colonial Hills Elementary
Houston, TX

SCENES OF SYMMETRY

Students' symmetry skills take shape right before your eyes with this picture-perfect project! First, demonstrate how to cut an object (like a heart) from folded paper. Show students the unfolded cutout and explain that when objects are cut out in this way, the fold line is a line of symmetry. Then have students cut out a variety of shapes from folded paper scraps, unfold the shapes, and use their pencils to trace the lines of symmetry. As a finale, have each child design a scene of symmetry. To do this, a student cuts out colorful symmetrical shapes that relate to a specific setting; then he glues the cutouts on a sheet of construction paper, creating a desired scene. Display the projects with the title "Scenes of Symmetry."

Amanda Dolan
Walpole, MA

ANSWER KEY

Symmetrical	Not Symmetrical
A B C D E H I K M O Q T U V W X Y	F G J L N P R S

ALPHABET SYMMETRY

Symmetry in the alphabet? You bet! Use this math center to convince students of this fascinating fact. Store a set of vinyl or felt uppercase letter cutouts in a resealable plastic bag. Place the bag of letters, a supply of paper, an answer key, and pencils at the center. A student draws a line of symmetry on his paper and labels the two resulting columns "Symmetrical" and "Not Symmetrical." Next, he removes the letters from the bag. He bends each letter cutout in several directions to determine whether it is symmetrical; then he writes the letter on his paper in the appropriate column. When all the letters have been examined, he uses the answer key to check his work. Don't be surprised if students request to inspect a set of lowercase letters too!

Diane Fortunato—Gr. 2
Carteret School
Bloomfield, NJ

SYMMETRICAL DESIGNS

Reinforce symmetry with this partner activity! To begin, each student draws a line of symmetry on a sheet of one-inch graph paper. Then he uses crayons to color a desired design on one side of the symmetry line. Next, each student trades places with a classmate—leaving his design and his crayons at his desk. Each child now carefully colors his partner's paper so that a symmetrical design results. Allow time at the end of the activity for each twosome to evaluate its designs for accuracy. Keep a supply of graph paper on hand! You can count on students being eager to repeat this partner activity again and again.

adapted from an idea by Donna Urbach
Muscoda, WI

INVESTIGATING ANGLES

Angles are everywhere, and that's exactly what this activity teaches youngsters! Tell students you are sending them on an angle investigation. To prepare, have every student label a sheet of drawing paper for each angle he is investigating. Then give each child a discarded magazine, and ask him to cut out examples of each angle and glue them on the appropriate paper. Compile the students' completed projects into a class book titled "Getting the Angle on Angles." To extend the learning, invite students to investigate their surroundings for examples of angles, and set aside time for the students to describe the angles they've seen.

Carol Perks
Miami, FL

ANGLE WORKOUT

Create additional interest in angles with this movement activity. On the chalkboard draw and label a *right angle* (90°), an *acute angle* (less than 90°) and an *obtuse angle* (more than 90° and less than 180°). Then challenge each child to sit on the floor and form a right angle. To do this, she extends her legs out in front of her, keeps her back straight, and extends her arms straight above her head. Next, direct the students to adjust their angle formations according to your oral directions. To form an acute angle, a student leans forward. To form an obtuse angle, she leans back. "Obtuse! Right! Obtuse! Acute!" Who knew a lesson on angles could be such great exercise?

Debbie Murphy
Goodnoe Elementary
Holland, PA

GEOMETRY BOOK CORNER
Get a whole new angle on geometry with these kid-pleasing literature connections!

When a Line Bends...A Shape Begins
Written by Rhonda Gowler Greene
Illustrated by James Kaczman

Three Pigs, One Wolf, and Seven Magic Shapes
Written by Grace Maccarone
Illustrated by David Neuhaus
Math Activities by Marilyn Burns

Shape Up!:
Fun With Triangles and Other Polygons
Written by David A. Adler
Illustrated by Nancy Tobin

Sir Cumference and the First Round Table
Written by Cindy Neuschwander
Illustrated by Wayne Geehan

So Many Circles, So Many Squares
Written & Photographed by Tana Hoban

Shapes, Shapes, Shapes
Written & Photographed by Tana Hoban

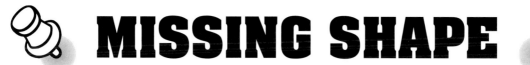

MISSING SHAPE

Name of shape: ______________________________

Description of shape: ______________________________

____

____

____

This shape has been seen posing as ______________________________

____

____

____

____

Information provided by Detective ______________________________

Note to the teacher: Use with "Shape Detectives" on page 47.

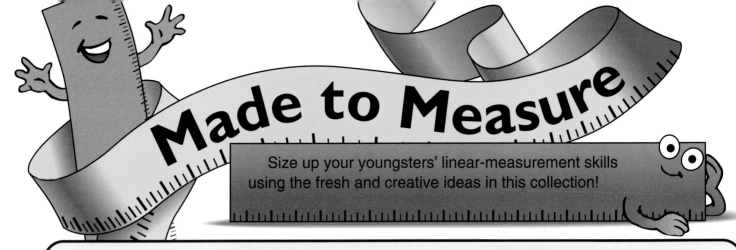

Made to Measure

Size up your youngsters' linear-measurement skills using the fresh and creative ideas in this collection!

How Big?

Fe! Fi! Fo! Fum! Set the stage for some giant-size measuring with an oral reading of *Jack and the Beanstalk*! Then divide the class into six small groups. Provide each group with a length of bulletin board paper, construction paper scraps, markers or crayons, glue, and scissors. Ask the members of each group to use their supplies and imaginations to make a part of the giant's body. Ask two different groups to make one arm each and two different groups to make one leg each. Ask one group to make the giant's head and another to make his body.

When the projects are ready, assemble the giant. Invite students to talk about the giant's comical appearance. Next, help volunteers measure different parts of the giant's body. Write these measurements on the giant so that students can study and compare them. Invite students to suggest how they could collectively make a giant that is more uniform in size. No doubt students will agree that this time a giant-size *measurement* project is in order!

Tami Bertini—Gr. 1
Gladbrook Elementary

Book of Measures

Oodles of opportunities for measuring are packed into this nifty booklet project! Give each child a construction paper booklet that holds five copies of page 58. Have each child write her name and "Book of Measures" on the front cover. Also have her complete the title of the first booklet page by writing "Our School" on the line provided. Next, take students on a guided tour of the school. Provide time for each child to measure and record in her booklet the length, width, and height of five or more items. For a fun follow-up, ask each child to state the measurements for the largest or smallest item she measured.

Instruct each child to complete the remaining pages of her booklet at home. To do this, she titles each page so that it describes the area, item, pet, or person she is measuring. Ask students to return their completed booklets to school on or before a designated date. When the booklets are returned, set aside time for students to share several of the measurements they've taken!

Melody Shaw
Carrollton, MS

For Good Measure

Sharpen measurement *and* writing skills with this partner activity. Pair students and confirm that each twosome has a ruler, a pencil, and a sheet of paper. Instruct each duo to measure the length of six classroom items of its own choosing. For each measured item, the pair composes a descriptive sentence that includes the gathered measurements. Next, have each pair exchange papers with another twosome, find each item described on the paper, and verify the measurements that were taken. Instruct students to star each verified sentence. Then, after a set amount of time, ask that the papers be returned to the students who wrote them. Students will enjoy choosing what they measure as well as confirming the measurements taken by their peers. Better plan to repeat this activity a few times for good measure!

Amy Emmons—Gr. 2
Enon Elementary
Franklinton, LA

Rodger and Chen

1. The purple and green tissue box on Ms. Emmons's desk is 4 inches wide and 5 inches tall.

2. The bright orange welcome sign on the classroom door is 10 inches long and 8 inches wide.

3.

A Royal Predicament

Rolf Myller's *How Big Is a Foot?* is a must for your measurement unit! In this delightful romp, a king decides to give the queen a bed for her birthday. Because beds have not yet been invented, no one is quite sure how large the bed should be. The king provides the answer—three feet by six feet. Read the story aloud, stopping when the apprentice learns the dimensions of the bed. Divide the class into small groups and give each group a length of bulletin board paper on which to design a quilt for the queen's bed. Ask each group to select an apprentice who will use the king's technique of using his own feet to measure the size of the group's quilt. Allow plenty of time for each group to measure, cut out, and decorate its quilt. Display the completed quilts so that the tops are level. Ask students to study the quilts and suggest why all the quilts are not the same size. Invite students to predict how their measurement experiences might play out in the story. Then read aloud the remainder of *How Big Is a Foot?* At the book's completion, students are sure to better understand why a standard system of measurement is essential!

Judy M. Christiansen
Harlan, IA

Community Planners

Merge math and social studies curricula when you challenge students to collectively construct a community named Measurementville! Post the name of the community on a bulletin board. Then have students craft construction paper components for the community that include buildings, homes, cars, streets, scenery, and people. Explain that each item must be measured and labeled accordingly before it can become a part of Measurementville. The final result is a picture-perfect review of linear measurement that provides a sense of community!

Gina Zimecki—Gr. 2
Bernice Young Elementary School
Burlington, NJ

On the Move

Students take their rulers on the road for this hands-on measurement activity! At each of several centers, provide five like items of varying sizes to be measured. Consider items such as books, pencils, tagboard strips, pipe cleaners, and so on. Assign a letter to each center and then number the items at each center from 1 to 5. During his assigned center time, a child heads to a center with his ruler, his pencil, and a recording sheet like the one shown. He measures the length of each item at the center, records his findings on his paper, and then moves on to another center. When he has measured each item in every center, he returns to his desk. If desired, store an answer key or two at your desk and invite students to use the keys to check the measurements they gathered. Now, that's a measurement activity that brings students to their feet!

June Shaner—Gr. 2
Our Lady of Fatima School
Lakewood, CO

Name Nick

Measurement Centers

Center A	Center B
Pencils	Pipe Cleaners
1.	1.
2.	2.
3.	3.
4.	4.
5.	5.

Cuddly Calibrations

For this warm and fuzzy measurement activity, ask each child to bring to school a favorite stuffed toy. Be sure to have a few extra stuffed critters on hand. You will also need several tape measures. To begin, each child traces the outline of her critter onto a provided length of bulletin board paper and colors the resulting outline to resemble her cuddly companion. Next, she uses her ruler (and a tape measure when necessary) to measure her fuzzy friend. She labels her illustration with the measurements she gathers. Display the resulting posters in the hallway for everyone to see.

adapted from an idea by
Angie Lamb—Chapter 1
Rutledge Elementary School
Rutledge, TN

Spaghetti and Meatballs

Continue to whet your youngsters' appetites for measurement at this mouth-watering center! Cut ten meatball shapes from construction paper and label them in alphabetical order from *A* through *J.* Securely tape to the back of each cutout one end of a length of string (spaghetti). Vary the string lengths. To create an answer key, measure each string from the edge of the meatball to its unattached end. Trim the string to a desired measurement and record this measurement on the answer key.

Store the meatballs and spaghetti in a bowl or cooking pot. Place the bowl, a ruler, a yardstick, a supply of paper, and the answer key at a center. A student measures the spaghetti lengths and records his answers in alphabetical order on his paper. Then he uses the answer key to check his work. For added fun, place a recording of Tomie dePaola's *Strega Nona* at a different center for your youngsters' listening pleasure! Your students' interest in pasta is sure to grow!

Paula Beckerman
Arlington, TX

By the Tail

You can count on an enthusiastic response to this unique measurement activity! Copy page 59 onto construction paper. Cut the cards apart and place them in a container. Place the container of cards at a center along with two rolls of adding machine tape, a ruler, a yardstick, pencils, scissors, and markers or crayons. Inform students that each card is labeled with the name of an animal and the approximate length of its tail. Arrange for students to visit the center in pairs. A pair removes a card from the container and measures and cuts a length of adding machine tape that is the length of the animal's tail. Next, the duo writes on the paper the length of the tape and the name of the animal. Then the pair places the card in a discard pile.

As student pairs complete their work at the center, post their strips on a bulletin board so that a bar graph is created. After every student has completed the center with a partner, invite interested students to revisit the center to complete any remaining cards. When the graph is intact, pose a series of measurement-related questions for students to answer.

Karrie Jayne Johnson—Gr. 3
Joseph C. Caruso School
Keansburg, NJ

57

Measuring _____

Object	Length	Width	Height
1.			
2.			
3.			
4.			
5.			
6.			
7.			
8.			
9.			
10.			

Note to the teacher: Use with "Book of Measures" on page 54.

lion	36 inches		sea otter	15 inches
bobcat	8 inches		gray wolf	24 inches
gray squirrel	10 inches		cheetah	24 inches
hamster	2 inches		Arctic hare	5 inches
red kangaroo	36 inches		gray fox	12 inches
giant anteater	35 inches		aardvark	24 inches
North American beaver	18 inches		coyote	16 inches
jaguar	30 inches		three-toed sloth	3 inches
llama	6 inches		blue monkey	30 inches
snow leopard	36 inches		raccoon	13 inches

Once Upon a Time...

An Enchanting Collection of Time-Telling Activities

With favorite fairy-tale characters by your side, spin a tale of time-telling practice that has a delightfully happy ending!

contributions by Bonnie Baumgras, Las Vegas, NV

Knock! Knock!

Open a door to continued practice matching digital and analog times! Make a construction paper copy of page 62 for each child. Laminate the copies and use an X-acto knife to slit the dotted lines on each copy. Give each child a page of prepared patterns, a brad, and access to clear tape. A student cuts out the clock hands and then cuts along the bold lines. To assemble the manipulative, she pokes the brad through the dot on the short clock hand, the long clock hand, and the clock face (in that order); then she fastens the brad. Next, she inserts strip A into its matching set of slits, overlaps the ends of the strip, and secures them with tape. She repeats this step with strips B and C.

To use her manipulative, she adjusts the strips and the clock hands so that the same time appears on both. Every day, pose different fairy-tale scenarios (see provided samples) and have students show the corresponding times on their clock manipulatives.

Candi DeFran, East River Elementary, Grosse Ile, MI

Sample scenarios:
Mama Bear poured porridge at 3:30.
Goldilocks ate Baby Bear's porridge at 4:14.
Papa Bear took a nap at 6:00.

Time to Climb!

Fe! Fi! Fo! Fum! Keep page 63 handy, and your youngsters' time-telling skills are sure to keep growing and growing and growing! For each time-telling review, make a copy of the page and then program the copy to reinforce a desired time-telling skill (such as time to the half hour or time to the quarter hour) by drawing clock hands or by writing digital times on the lines. Provide oral student directions or program the cloud with one of the following: "Write the time on the lines below each clock" or "Draw hands on each clock to show the time that is given." Now, that's golden assessment!

A Day in the Life

Add a fairy-tale twist to a review of A.M. and P.M. times! On the board write a student-generated list of fairy-tale characters. Have each child copy a name from the board onto his paper and then list eight activities the character might do at different times during a day: four before noon and four after noon. Next, have each student fold a 6" x 18" strip of light-colored construction paper in half (to 6" x 9"). Have him title the resulting front cover "A Day in the Life of [character's name]" and add a desired cover illustration. Also give each child two copies of the clock cards from page 64 (for a total of eight cards).

To make a timeline of his character's day, a student unfolds his paper. He uses a crayon to trace over the fold line and to label the left half of the paper "A.M." and the right half "P.M." Next, he completes a clock card for each activity by programming the clock with the time the activity will be completed, writing the corresponding digital time in the box, and describing the activity on the lines. Then he cuts out the completed cards and glues them in chronological order on the appropriate halves of his paper. Be sure to set aside time for students to share their projects with the class.

A Quarter Past 12

Cinderella can lend students a hand learning fractional measurements of time! For each child make a construction paper copy of the clock and clock hand patterns from page 64. Laminate the copies for durability and then give each student a brad and a set of patterns. Have each child cut out the clock hands and then cut along the bold lines. To assemble her clock, she pokes the brad through the dot on the short clock hand, the long clock hand, and the clock face (in that order); then she fastens the brad.

Ask students to explain the significance of the quarters. Lead them to conclude that each quarter (or one-fourth) of the clock face is labeled with a quarter. Then have each child position the hands on his clock to show a series of times that include *quarter past, quarter to,* and *half past* (explaining that two quarters equal a half). Have students keep the clocks handy for additional time-telling practice that includes fractional measurements of time.

Michele Repass—Gr. 2, Hugh Mercer Elementary, Fredericksburg, VA

Wolf Whereabouts

Monitoring the actions of the big bad wolf is definitely a task for student pairs! Each child needs her clock manipulative from "A Quarter Past 12" (or something similar). To begin, pose the following problem: "The big bad wolf got up at 7:30 (or half past seven). He had practiced huffing and puffing for 20 minutes when the phone rang. What time did the phone ring?" Challenge each twosome to use one or both of its clocks to solve the problem. Then invite students to share how they determined that the phone rang at 7:50. Continue posing a variety of problems for students to solve. If desired, have each pair record its answers on paper. See "That Wolf!" for some problems to get you started.

Pam Crane

That Wolf!

The big bad wolf sees a little pig leave its house at 3:10. He sees the same pig return at 3:45. How long has the pig been gone?

At 8:30 the big bad wolf will meet a little pig at the apple orchard. If it takes the wolf 25 minutes to get to the orchard, what time must he leave to arrive at the orchard on time?

The three little pigs invite the big bad wolf to have lunch with them at 11:45. The wolf arrives seven minutes early. What time does the wolf arrive?

Patterns

Use with "Knock! Knock!" on page 60.

A		
12		
11	B	C
10	5	9
9	4	8
8	3	7
7	2	6
6	1	5
5	0	4
4		3
3		2
2		1
1		0

Please return at...

A : B C

Name _____

Time to Climb!

_____ : _____   _____ : _____   _____ : _____   _____ : _____

_____ : _____   _____ : _____   _____ : _____   _____ : _____

_____ : _____   _____ : _____

Bonus Box: Choose a time from this page. On the back of this paper, write a sentence that tells what the giant is doing at this exact time. Include the time in your sentence.

Note to the teacher: Use with "Time to Climb!" on page 60.

Clock Cards and Patterns

Use the clock cards with "A Day in the Life" on page 61.

Use the patterns with "A Quarter Past 12" on page 61.

Time Races On!

From slow and steady to fast and furious, this timely collection of activities is just what your students need to race ahead to perfect time-telling skills. So what are you waiting for? There's no time like the present to get started!

GO, TURTLE!

King-Size Clock

With this unique clock, interest in time-telling practice will be at an all-time high! In advance spray-paint a clock face that includes numbers, minute markings, and a center dot (to indicate placement of the clock hands) on a solid-color king-size bedsheet. To practice time-telling skills, place the sheet in an open area, and have students sit around the lower half of the clock face. Position a yardstick as the minute hand and a ruler as the hour hand, and ask students to state the time shown. Then invite each student, in turn, to manipulate the clock hands as you announce varying times. When the activity is completed, simply fold the sheet for easy storage. Now, that's a king-size idea!

Gina Black—Gr. 2, Remsen-Union Elementary, Remsen, IA

Hooray Hare!
Hop 15 times.
less than a minute: 𝍸
a minute: |
more than a minute: ||
Draw 20 circles.
less than a minute: 𝍸 |||
a minute:
more than a minute:
Write the principal's name ten times.
less than a minute:
a minute: |
more than a minute: 𝍸 ||

Just a Minute

A *minute* is a *minute* is a *minute*—but how long is a *minute?* This partner activity helps students explore the length of 60 seconds. For every two students, create a task card (similar to the ones shown) that features a different activity. First, ask students to sit quietly for one minute. Then lead the class in an activity, such as clapping or humming, for one minute. Have students describe how these two minutes were alike and/or different.

Next, pair students and give each twosome a task card. On your signal, one partner in each pair performs the activity on the pair's card while the other partner observes. Announce when one minute is over. Allow time for those students who are still performing to complete their tasks and for each observer to record the outcome of the activity on the pair's task card. Then have the twosomes trade task cards and the partners switch roles for another round of fun. Continue in this manner until each pair has performed each activity. Conclude the lesson by having each twosome total the tally marks in each category on its final task card. After each pair has shared the tallied information with the class, invite students to tell what they have learned about a minute of time. Doesn't time fly when you're having fun?

Susan Majors—Grs. 1–2, Palmer Lake Elementary, Palmer Lake, CO

Individual Timepieces

These individual practice clocks will provide you with instant feedback on your students' time-telling skills. On tagboard duplicate a class supply of open clock-face patterns (if desired, enlarge the clock-face pattern on page 69 for this purpose). Laminate and cut out each clock; then give each child a clock, a wipe-off marker, and a tissue. To begin, announce a time. A student draws clock hands on his clock to show the announced time; then he displays his programmed clock for your approval. A quick glance can assess each student's efforts. Then have each student wipe off the clock hands with his tissue and prepare to reprogram his clock. What a nifty way to provide youngsters with hands-on time-telling practice!

Jill D. Hamilton—Gr. 1, Schoeneck Elementary, Stevens, PA

Pam Crane

Wild and Wacky Wristwatches

Watch out! This interactive bulletin board will have students showing off their time-telling skills! Give each student an index card labeled with a different time. To make a jumbo wristwatch, a student designs a clock face that shows her designated time on a thin white paper plate. Next, she personalizes and decorates two 6" x 18" strips of construction paper to resemble watchbands. Then she glues the watchbands to the paper plate as shown. Encourage students to further customize their watches as desired. Next, have each student write her name on the back of her index card. Mount each wristwatch on a bulletin board labeled "Watch Our Wristwatches!" Place the index cards and pushpins in a container near the display. A student matches each digital time on a card to a wristwatch, flips the card to verify her match, and then uses a pushpin to suspend the card near the wristwatch. When the student completes the activity, she returns the pushpins and index cards to the provided container.

Jill D. Hamilton—Gr. 1

Turtle Time

These individual turtle tachistoscopes provide students with practice matching digital and analog times. On construction paper duplicate the turtle pattern and the two tachistoscope strips on page 69 to make a class supply. Using an X-acto knife, slit the dotted lines on each turtle. To make a turtle tachistoscope, a student colors his turtle pattern; then he cuts out his turtle and both strips. He programs each clock face to show a different time before he randomly writes the corresponding digital times on the second strip. Then he inserts the strips into the turtle as shown.

To use his tachistoscope, the student adjusts the strips to match. Set aside time for students to exchange and complete their classmates' projects.

Susan Majors—Grs. 1–2, Palmer Lake Elementary, Palmer Lake, CO

TURTLE!

Got the Time?

These fashionable timepieces make telling time fun! Duplicate the clock pattern (page 69) onto tagboard to make a class supply. Laminate and cut out each clock. Hole-punch the top of each clock; then thread a length of yarn through the hole and tie the yarn's ends. Next, divide the cutouts into sets of five and use a wipe-off marker to program each set with a different time.

Each morning, randomly distribute the timepieces. Then, throughout the day, incorporate the times shown on the timepieces into your daily activities. For example, request that students wearing the time 6:30 line up first for lunch or that students wearing matching times form small groups. At the end of the week, reprogram each set of five clocks with a different time, and you'll be ready for more telling-time fun the following week.

Jill D. Hamilton—Gr. 1, Schoeneck Elementary, Stevens, PA

Day and Night

Review A.M. and P.M. times with this eye-opening activity. Have each student fold a 12" x 18" sheet of drawing paper in half, unfold his paper, and draw a line down the middle. On the left half of his paper, a student writes an A.M. time and illustrates what he might be doing at that time. On the right half of his paper, he writes a P.M. time and illustrates what he might be doing at that time. Set aside time for interested students to share their projects with their classmates.

Susan Majors—Grs. 1–2, Palmer Lake Elementary, Palmer Lake, CO

HARE!

7 A.M.   8 P.M.

Time Check!

Reinforce time-telling skills with daily time checks. At five different times during the day, spontaneously declare, "Time Check!" Each child stops what he is doing and writes the time on a paper strip or a duplicated recording sheet. Be sure to make note of the times yourself. At the end of each day, announce the times that should be listed on the students' papers. Now, that's easy timekeeping practice!

Diane Balkcom—Gr. 3, Summers Elementary School, Lake City, FL

It's About Time!

This class-book project reinforces that telling time is an important life skill. Challenge students to name occupations that can be performed only by people who can tell time. As you list each child's suggestion on the chalkboard, ask the student to explain his choice. For example, a student might suggest a bus driver who must stay on a time schedule or a nurse who must give patients medicines at designated times. Next have each youngster choose a different occupation from the list. On provided paper have him illustrate himself performing the job and write a sentence or two explaining why he must know how to tell time. Bind the completed projects between two construction paper covers and title the resulting class book "The Times of Our Lives!"

Jennie D'Assisi, Richmond Hill, Ontario, Canada

A teacher needs to know when to take her students to lunch.

A coach needs to know how much time is left in the game.

It's a Match!

This large-group game helps youngsters master time-telling skills lickety-split! For every two students, program an open clock card (patterns on page 70) with a different time; then, for each clock card, label an index card with the matching digital time. Laminate the cards for durability. To play, randomly distribute the game cards. Each student reads the time on his game card and searches for the classmate who has the same time. When two students discover that their game cards match, they sit down. After each student has found his match, collect and shuffle the game cards; then play the game again!

Jill D. Hamilton—Gr. 1, Schoeneck Elementary, Stevens, PA

A Line of Times

Time keeps on ticking with this partner activity! Give each student a copy of the eight open clock cards on page 70. Have each student cut out and program each clock card with a different time; then pair the students and give each pair a 30-inch length of yarn. Each twosome places its yarn in a horizontal line to represent a timeline that starts at 12:00. Then the pair stacks its combined cards facedown. In turn each student draws a clock card and places it in sequential order on the timeline. If a student draws a card with a time that has already been played, he places the card on top of its duplicate. After checking each group's timeline, have students sort their cards, change partners, and repeat the activity. Tick-tock, tick-tock!

Marsha Rogers, Lincoln Elementary School, Ardmore, OK

Timely Journals

Save time each day for students to write in time-related journals. To make a journal for each student, staple a supply of the journal page on page 70 between two construction paper covers. Each day, a student completes a journal page. To do this she writes a day and/or date, her favorite time from that day, and a reason for choosing that time. She also draws hands on the clock face that show the favorite time she has written about. From time to time, invite students to share their journal entries with their classmates.

Jill D. Hamilton—Gr. 1

Time to Evaluate

As you wind down your study of time, use page 71 to assess each youngster's time-telling skills. If further assessment is needed, reprogram a copy of the page with five different time-related events for students to complete.

My favorite time of the day on
Monday, Dec. 8,
was _3:30_.
I liked this time because _my ballet teacher told me I was doing very well._

Jill D. Hamilton—Gr. 1

Use the turtle and tachistoscope strips with "Turtle Time" on page 66.

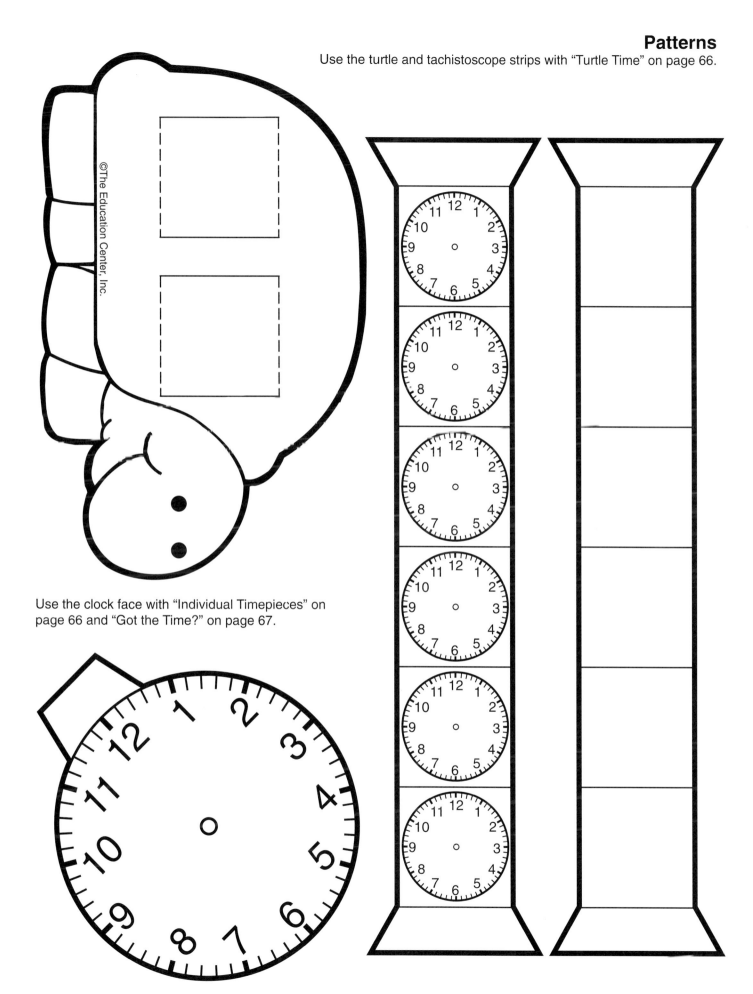

Use the clock face with "Individual Timepieces" on page 66 and "Got the Time?" on page 67.

My favorite time of the day on

_____

was _____.

I liked this time because _____

_____

_____

_____

_____.

Note to the teacher: Use the clock cards with "It's a Match!" and "A Line of Times" on page 68. Use the journal page with "Timely Journals" on page 68.

Name_____

What's the Time?

Read each sentence.
Write a time on the lines.
Show the time on the clock.

1. This is the time I wake up.	____ : ____	(clock face)
2. This is the time the school day begins.	____ : ____	(clock face)
3. This is the time I eat lunch.	____ : ____	(clock face)
4. This is the time the school day ends.	____ : ____	(clock face)
5. This is the time I go to bed.	____ : ____	(clock face)

Bonus Box: On the back of this paper, write a sentence that tells about a time. Then draw a clock that shows the time you wrote about.

©The Education Center, Inc. • *The Best of* The Mailbox® *Math* • *Book 2* • TEC1491

Note to the teacher: Use with "Time to Evaluate" on page 68.

71

Right on the Money!

Looking for a way to reinforce students' money skills? Cash in on this rich collection of teacher-tested ideas. You can bet your bottom dollar that a "swine" time will be had by all!

ideas contributed by Anne M. Bosarge and Jill Hamilton

Coin Collections

To complete the activities in this unit, each student needs a collection of coins. For easy management give each child a personalized envelope (or resealable plastic bag) to serve as a wallet, and a set of imitation coins to store inside. If you prefer real coins, request in a note to parents that each child bring a specific set of coins to school for this purpose.

Money, Dough, or Moolah?

Get your money unit off to a profitable start with this intriguing activity. Show students a dollar bill and a handful of coins. Ask students what these items are called and write their responses on the chalkboard. Broaden your youngsters' vocabularies by adding to the list some less familiar names for money, like *sawbacks, moolah, greenbacks, bread, bucks, oof, gelt, bits, skins,* and *cabbage.* Then, for added fun, share several money expressions from the provided list and challenge students to determine the meaning of each one.

Money Expressions

"A dime a dozen"
"Your bottom dollar"
"Two cents' worth"
"A penny for your thoughts"
   "Time is money."
   "Money talks."
   "Money doesn't grow on trees."
"Show me the money!"
"A fool and his money are soon parted."
"The love of money is the root of all evil."
"Money can't buy happiness."
"Penny-pincher"
"You look like a million bucks!"
"A penny saved is a penny earned."
"Nickel-and-diming"

Kimberly Richard

Profitable Patterns

If your students need practice identifying coins, this patterning activity is a wise investment! Pair students and give each partner an identical set of coins. In turn, each student uses his coin set to create a pattern; then his partner uses his set of coins to continue the pattern. Next, the two students work together to state the name and value of each coin in the pattern they created. To increase the difficulty of the task, have each student pair determine the total value of each completed pattern. Wow! Who would have thought coin patterns could be so profitable!

The Banker Says...

Reinforce coin-recognition and listening skills with this variation of the popular game Simon Says. Give each small group a penny, nickel, dime, and quarter for every group member except one. (For example, a group of six students will receive five of each coin.) Ask each group to randomly arrange its coins on a playing surface. Also select one member in each group to be the banker. To play, a banker tells his group to pick up a specific coin. The group members should respond only if the banker's request is prefaced by "The banker says." After the banker has verified the coins that were selected, the coins are returned to the playing surface. A student who chooses an incorrect coin or who responds without the banker's okay sits out for one round of play. After a designated amount of game time, appoint a different banker for each group and resume play. Continue in this manner until each group member has been the banker. Now, that's a game plan you can take to the bank!

Pick up a quarter.

Days of the Week	Number of Pockets	1¢ Pocket Value	5¢ Pocket Value
Monday	48	48¢	$2.40
Tuesday	60	60¢	$3.00

Pocket Change

Cash in with this daily small-group activity! Give each group a supply of pennies and ask each child to put one penny in each pocket she is wearing. Next, have the students remove the pennies from their pockets and determine the cash value of each group member's pockets and the cash value of the entire group's pockets. Then assist the class in finding the total cash value of all the students' pockets. For older students, extend the activity by challenging the small groups to determine similar totals based on a pocket value of five or ten cents. If desired, record this information on a chart like the one shown. Plan to repeat the activity every few days during your study of money. No doubt your youngsters' money skills will grow right along with the number of pockets they are wearing!

Breaking the Bank!

Oink! Oink! This small-group game provides plenty of practice with coin identification. On pink construction paper, duplicate a class supply of the piggy-bank pattern on page 77. Laminate and cut out the piggy banks. Also make a spinner wheel (like the one shown) for each group. Divide the class into small groups. Give each group a spinner wheel, a sharpened pencil, and a large paper clip to use as a spinner. Then give each group member a piggy-bank cutout and a predetermined number of coins to place on her bank. (The total value of the coins may vary, but the *number* of coins must be the same.)

To play, each player in turn spins the spinner and removes from her bank the coin that matches the value she has spun. She places this coin in a personal discard pile. If a student spins the pig, she acts like a little pig and puts the coins from her discard pile back in her bank. The first player to empty her bank wins the game!

Dollar Details

Because the dollar bill is used more frequently than any other paper money, it has the shortest life span—only 18 months. During that time, a dollar bill changes hands an average of 400 times! Use "The Dollar Song" and "Dollar Booklet" on this page to reinforce the value of this very popular greenback.

The Dollar Song
(sung to the tune of "Ten Little Indians")

10 little, 20 little, 30 little pennies.
40 little, 50 little, 60 little pennies.
70 little, 80 little, 90 little pennies.
100 pennies make a dollar!

2 small, 4 small, 6 small nickels.
8 small, 10 small, 12 small nickels.
14 small, 16 small, 18 small nickels.
20 nickels make a dollar!

1 tiny, 2 tiny, 3 tiny dimes.
4 tiny, 5 tiny, 6 tiny dimes.
7 tiny, 8 tiny, 9 tiny dimes.
10 dimes make a dollar!

1 big, 2 big, 3 big quarters.
4 big, 4 big, 4 big quarters.
1 big, 2 big, 3 big quarters.
4 quarters make a dollar!

Rebecca Brudwick—Gr. 1
Hoover Elementary School
North Mankato, MN

Dollar Booklet

Here's a great way for students to make some bucks and brush up on their money skills too! To make a dollar booklet, a student stacks three 8½" x 11" sheets of white paper and holds the pages vertically. He slides the top sheet upward approximately one inch and the bottom sheet downward approximately one inch. Next, the student folds his papers forward to create six graduated layers or pages; then he staples the resulting booklet close to the fold. The student writes the title "[Student's name]'s Dollar Booklet" on the cover and labels the bottoms of the booklet pages as shown. To complete his booklet, he illustrates the dollar bill and stamps the appropriate coin impressions on the corresponding booklet pages.

Shari Sullivan Marshall, Crested Butte, CO

$1 $1
$1 $1

dollar bill
quarters
dimes
nickels
pennies

21¢

Money March

Students march toward better money-counting skills with this game plan! To make a trail of coins like the one shown, enlarge the coin patterns on page 77 and duplicate a supply of each coin on an appropriate color of paper. Laminate and cut out the coins; then tape a path of cut-outs on the floor. (Store the extra coins for later use.) Post the cash value of the coin path in a designated location. A student orally adds the coin values as he marches alongside the path. Then he verifies his cash total with the one that you've posted. Modify the coin path every few days, re-membering to post its corresponding cash value each time. You can count on improved money-counting skills in no time!

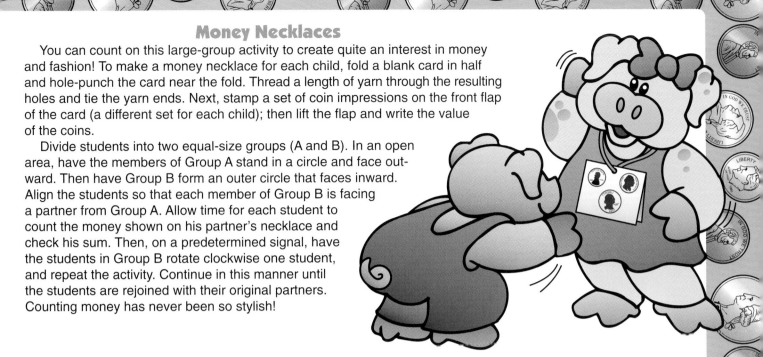

Money Necklaces

You can count on this large-group activity to create quite an interest in money and fashion! To make a money necklace for each child, fold a blank card in half and hole-punch the card near the fold. Thread a length of yarn through the resulting holes and tie the yarn ends. Next, stamp a set of coin impressions on the front flap of the card (a different set for each child); then lift the flap and write the value of the coins.

Divide students into two equal-size groups (A and B). In an open area, have the members of Group A stand in a circle and face outward. Then have Group B form an outer circle that faces inward. Align the students so that each member of Group B is facing a partner from Group A. Allow time for each student to count the money shown on his partner's necklace and check his sum. Then, on a predetermined signal, have the students in Group B rotate clockwise one student, and repeat the activity. Continue in this manner until the students are rejoined with their original partners. Counting money has never been so stylish!

Money Spin-Off

Take students' money-counting skills for a spin! For this large-group activity, use your overhead projector to display a transparent spinner for class viewing. To make the spinner, visually divide a transparent circle into four sections and program each section with a different coin value. Then, using a fastener, snap a loose spinner in the center of the wheel. Each student will need a supply of coins and a sheet of paper to use as a workmat. To begin the activity, spin the spinner. Announce the designated value and have each student place the corresponding coin on his workmat. Then spin again and have each student place this coin on his workmat. In between spins ask the students to tell you how much money they have collected. For easy counting, encourage students to reduce the number of coins on their workmats by continually exchanging coins of lesser value for those of higher value. Continue play until $1.00 or another predetermined amount is collected.

Once students are familiar with the activity, divide the class into two teams. Enlist one player from each team to be the team spinner. The team spinners alternately spin for cash amounts. The first team to collect a predetermined amount of cash wins the game.

Cups o' Coins

Cups of coins are great investments in your youngsters' money skills. Sequentially number one Styrofoam cup for every two students; then place coin sets of varying values in the cups. Pair students and give each twosome a cup of coins, a pencil, and a sheet of paper. One student in each pair sequentially numbers the paper to match the total number of coin cups created. Then each twosome gently spills its coins onto a work area, determines the cash value of the coins, and writes this amount on the paper beside the cup's number. On a signal from you, each pair passes its cup of coins to the next twosome along a designated route. The activity continues in this manner until each pair has counted and recorded a cash amount for each cup. What a "cent-sational" way to improve your youngsters' money-counting skills!

Bags of Money!

Shake up an interest in counting money with this partner activity. For every two students, place ten or more coins of various values in a paper lunch bag and fold down the top of the resulting money bag. Then pair students and give each twosome a money bag, and scrap paper and a pencil for keeping score. In turn, each partner shakes the money bag, reaches inside it without looking, and removes three coins. Next, each partner determines the total value of the coins he is holding. The student who has the higher money value earns one point for the round of play. Then both partners return their coins to the money bag, and another round of play begins. The player with the most points at the end of game time wins! As students perfect their money-counting skills, increase the number of coins they remove from the bag.

The Coin Exchange

Your young tycoons will jump at the chance to try their luck at the Coin Exchange. Pair students and give each twosome a die. Also give each student a duplicated gameboard similar to the one shown and the following coins: five pennies, two nickels, two dimes, and one quarter. To play, each partner in turn rolls the die. If a student rolls a five or less, she places an equivalent number of pennies atop the penny spaces on her gameboard. If she rolls a six, her turn is over. When a player fills all five penny spaces, she exchanges the pennies for a nickel. When she earns two nickels, she exchanges them for a dime, and so on. The first player who exchanges her coins for a quarter strikes it rich as the winner of the game!

The Piggy General Store

Reinforce students' money skills at a specialty store that accepts only piggy currency! Label a classroom area "The Piggy General Store." Stock this area with low-cost or donated items, such as paperback books, erasers, small toys, wrapped candies, posters, and pencils. Price each item—making sure to vary the prices so that some items will be easily affordable and others will require students to save their earnings. You will also need a toy cash register (or something similar) that you've stocked with duplicated piggy coins and dollars (see the patterns on page 78). Finally, post a sign that tells the days and times that the store will be open for business.

Next, have students suggest ways that they can earn spending money. Encourage ideas that reinforce positive behaviors, such as helping others, wearing school colors, sharing materials, and keeping a clean desk. Then list the students' ideas on poster board, and beside each item, indicate its cash reward. Display the resulting chart in a prominent classroom location.

Throughout your money unit, use piggy currency to reward your students' positive actions as outlined on the posted chart. If desired, have each student save his earnings in a resealable plastic bag. Students make desired purchases from The Piggy General Store during business hours. No doubt students will give this shopping experience three oinks!

Michelle McClanahan–Gr. 3, Christa McAuliffe Elementary, Lewisville, TX

Use the pig pattern with
"Breaking the Bank!" on
page 73.

Piggy Currency Patterns

Use with "The Piggy General Store" on page 76.

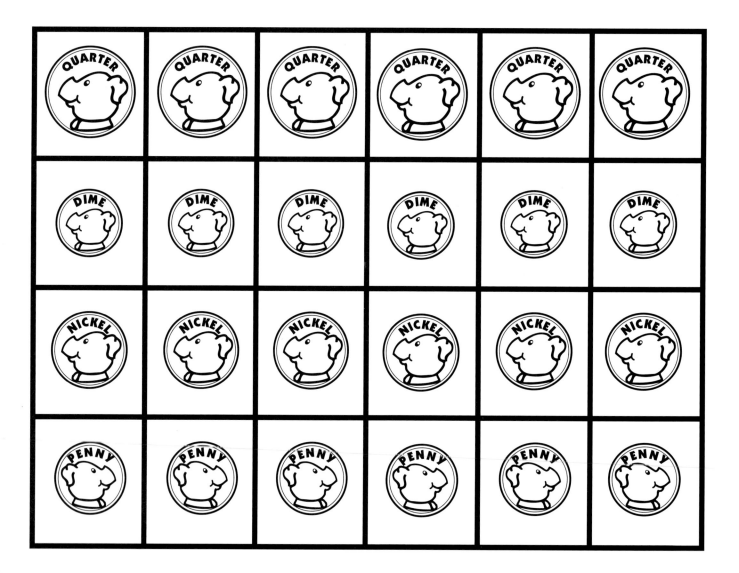

Grade A Graphing

Scatter these graphing activities throughout the school year and you'll have students who are "egg-cited" about math *and* each other!

ideas contributed by Monica Cavender

Clip It!

Students will have a grand time clipping their favorite choices on this easy-to-make clothespin graph! And, during the process, they'll learn plenty about each other! To make the graph, divide a strip of poster board into two columns. Program each column with dots and numbers (see illustration), setting up a one-to-one correspondence. Laminate the project for durability and then display it in a chalkboard tray. Several inches above the graph, write "I prefer..." Also give each child a personalized clothespin. Every morning, write a different choice above each column of the graph. When all students have clipped their preferences, have students interpret the data and answer questions about it. Later in the day, erase the choices for the day and ask a student helper to return the clothespins. Plan to repeat the activity (with two different choices) the following day!

Picturing Birthdays

Any way you slice it, this picture graph of student birthdays takes the cake! Program a 2' x 3' length of bulletin board paper with a chart listing the months of the year as shown. Showcase the grid against a backdrop of paper icing topped with paper candles and title the display "Happy Birthday!" Next, give each child a three-inch square of drawing paper. Have her write her initials in the top left corner, the date of her birthday (day only) in the lower right corner, and then draw her self-likeness in the center. One at a time, each child tapes her square on the graph for the correct month. Pose questions about the completed graph for students to answer. Keep the graph updated throughout the year by adding data when a new student enrolls and removing data when a student moves!

Patricia Nicome-Lendore—Gr. 1
Public School 221
Brooklyn, NY

Family Members	
0	
1	
2	
3	
4	
5	
6	
7	
8	
more	

Family Tallies

Count on plenty of enthusiasm when you ask students to tally family members and pets! Prepare four graphs like the one shown. Title the graphs "Family Members," "Sisters," "Brothers," and "Pets." If desired, laminate the graphs for reuse next year. Then hole-punch each graph about halfway down along the right edge. Securely tie one end of a yarn length through each hole. To the opposite end of each yarn length, tie a wipe-off crayon, making sure the crayon reaches the programmable areas of the graph. Display the graphs around the classroom. After a quick review of tally marks, ask each child to draw a tally mark beside the number (or word) on each graph that represents her family.

Discuss the results of the collected data. Ask students to identify the *range* and *mode* (the number most frequently represented) of each graph. Then have them compare the range and mode of all four graphs and determine why some are more similar than others. Conclude the activity by challenging students to determine the total number of family members (sisters, brothers, pets) in the entire class!

Favorite Colors

When youngsters compile their favorite colors on a class circle graph, the outcome is a one-of-a-kind color wheel! Cut out two large circles from white bulletin board paper. Draw a dot in the center of each one. Post one circle. Then divide the remaining circle into equal-size sections—one per child. Next, cut out the sections and distribute them. A child traces his cutout onto a sheet of construction paper that represents his favorite color and then cuts out the shape. Call students to the graph by favorite color and help each child in the group glue her colored cutout on the posted circle, keeping like colors together. Next, have students interpret the completed graph. For added fun, arrange for another class to complete the same activity so that the classes can compare their graphs.

Lost Teeth

Have a line on the number of student teeth that are lost during the year! On a large tooth cutout, design a grid like the one shown. Laminate the project for reuse next year, and then display it along with a strip of laminated poster board. Use a wipe-off marker to write the name of the current month on the strip. A student who loses a tooth during the month signs the strip. At the end of the month, enlist your students' help in counting the signatures (if any) and recording the data on the graph. Then wipe the poster board strip clean and reprogram it for the next month. Periodically provide graph-related questions for students to answer.

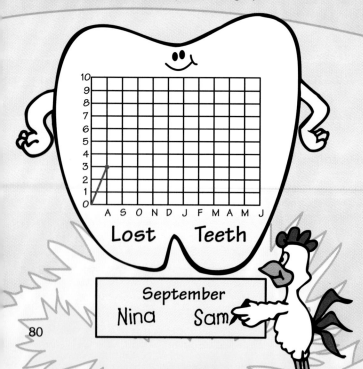

Lost Teeth

September
Nina   Sam

The Apples of Your Eye

Gather a bushel of information about your class with this "a-peel-ing" glyph project! Give each child a white construction paper copy of page 82. Read aloud the legend provided on this page, pausing after each listing so students may color their papers. Next, each child cuts out each leaf he colored and glues it near the stem of his apple. Then he cuts out the square and glues it on a nine-inch square of black construction paper. Showcase the framed apple portraits, an enlarged copy of the legend, and the title "The Apples of My Eye!" Each day provide a glyph-related question for students to investigate, such as "How many boys in our class like pizza?" or "How many girls in our class went to a different school last year?" Wow! These projects really do provide a bushel of facts!

Carol Horton
Taneytown, MD

On the Move

Vroom! Stay informed of your youngsters' afterschool travel plans with a transportation graph! Divide a two-foot square of bulletin board paper into quadrants and label the sections "Bus Riders," "Bike Riders," "Walkers," and "Other." Secure the graph to a magnetic surface like a chalkboard or the side of a filing cabinet. If desired, embellish the paper with cutouts and a border as shown. Next, cut a sheet of laminated poster board into small rectangles. Write each child's name on a different rectangle and attach a strip of magnetic tape to the back of each one. Display the collection of personalized markers near the graph. Each morning, a child places his marker in the quadrant that describes his afterschool travel plans. Shortly before the end of the day, ask a student to recap the graph for the class before he moves the markers off the graph. Bon voyage!

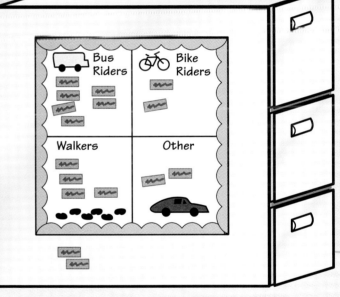

Legend

Apple
yellow = boy
red = girl

Hands
red = right-handed
yellow = left-handed

Book
purple = have a library card
orange = do not have a library card

Pencil
blue = have a sister or brother
red = do not have a sister or brother

Leaves
one green leaf = went to this school last year
two green leaves = went to a different school last year

Pencil eraser
pink = like pizza
yellow = do not like pizza

Stem
brown = do not have a pet
black = do have a pet

Yes or No

Use the Grade A reproducible activity on page 83 to assess how well students collect, organize, and interpret data! To create the same graphing activity for each child, make a copy of page 83, write a desired question in the question box, and then make a class supply of the page. To complete his activity, a child asks ten different people the programmed question. Each person he asks signs his paper and indicates a yes or no answer by coloring the appropriate egg. Next, the student organizes his data on the provided bar graph. Then he studies his completed graph and summarizes what he learned on the back of his paper. Set aside time for each child to share (compare) his findings with a small group of classmates.

For a variety of graphing projects, ask each child to program a blank copy of page 83 with his own yes/no question and then complete the activity. Have students report their findings to the class.

Patterns

Use with "The Apples of Your Eye" on page 81.

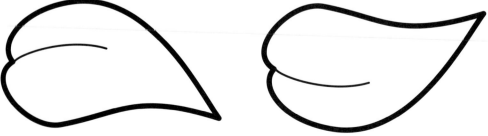

©The Education Center, Inc. • *The Best of* The Mailbox® *Math* • *Book 2* • TEC1491

Name _____

Grade A Graphing

First, collect data from ten different people.

Question

Names	Yes	No
1.		
2.		
3.		
4.		
5.		

Names	Yes	No
6.		
7.		
8.		
9.		
10.		

Next, organize your data on the bar graph.

Yes										
Yes										
No										

Now, study the bar graph. On the back of this paper, write two sentences that tell what you learned.

©The Education Center, Inc. • *The Best of The Mailbox® Math • Book 2 • TEC1491*

Note to the teacher: Use with "Yes or No" on page 81.

What Are the Odds?

An Introduction to Probability

Create a carnival-like atmosphere with these hands-on activities that double as an introduction to probability! Present one activity per day or plan a probability carnival during which students visit a series of adult-supervised learning stations. Either way, it's highly probable that plenty will be learned and a great time will be had by all!

ideas by Stacie Stone Davis

For Openers

Open your probability carnival with an activity that explores the concepts of *certain, probable* (or *likely*), *not probable* (or *not likely*), and *impossible.* Use alternating colors of paper to divide a bulletin board into five sections and then add the title and labels shown. When students have a clear understanding of the four posted terms, give each child a colorful balloon pattern on which you've written a different event. (See the provided list for suggestions.) Ask students to cut out the patterns. Then have each child, in turn, read aloud the event from his balloon and determine the probability that the event will occur for him. Then post the cutout on the display in the corresponding category.

Lead students to understand that probability is the chance or likelihood that an event will happen. Also help them conclude that the probability of an event occurring may not be the same for every person.

Events

You will feed an elephant today.
You will have homework tonight.
It will rain today.
You will read from a book today.
You will ride in an airplane this week.
You will eat ice cream this week.
It will snow this weekend.
You will have a birthday this month.
You will watch TV today.
You will ride a bus today.
The wind will blow today.
You will brush your teeth today.
You will get a phone call this week.
You will get a letter in the mail this week.

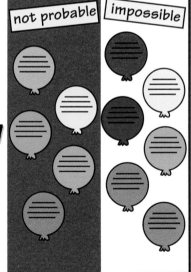

certain | probable | Welcome to the Probability Carnival! | not probable | impossible

Probability Pointers

Mathematically speaking, a probability is a ratio that tells how likely it is that an event will occur. The probability that a flipped coin will land on tails is 1:2—one chance in two that it will occur. The probability that a tossed die will reveal the number two is 1:6—one chance in six that a two will be rolled. It is doubtful that the results your youngsters gather will support expected probability. This is because the students are recording a small amount of data. The Law of Large Numbers maintains that a small number of trials will yield a wide range of results, which may or may not be close to the expected probability. On the other hand, a large number of trials will give results that are quite close to the expected probability. When investigating probability, it is important for students to understand that there are uncertainties and limitations involved when drawing conclusions from the data that is collected.

Go Fish!

A visit to the fishpond puts students in the swim with probability. To prepare, cover the sides of a large cardboard box with blue paper. Securely tie one end of a yarn length to a ruler and the other end to a horseshoe magnet. Then cut out 20 paper fish: ten green, six yellow, three blue, one red. Tape a paper clip to the mouth of each cutout.

As you put each color of fish in the pond, have students count the cutouts and record the information on a copy of "Go Fish!" from page 88. Next, have each child decide which color fish will be caught most often and write his prediction on his paper. (Clarify that each fish caught is immediately returned to the pond.) Then send pairs of students to the pond to test their predictions. For easy management, have Partner 1 fish and Partner 2 tend the pond. When Partner 1 catches a fish, he writes its color on his paper and then returns the fish to the pond. (If more than one fish is caught, he writes the color of the fish that appears to have been caught first.) Partner 2 mixes the fish in the pond and then Partner 1 resumes fishing. When Partner 1 has 20 catches recorded, he trades places with Partner 2, and they repeat the activity. Then each child uses his data to complete his paper.

When the entire class has gone fishing, ask students to share the results of their fishing expeditions. Use this data to make a class graph that shows the color of fish most frequently caught by your young anglers.

In a Spin

At this carnival game youngsters put a spin on probability! To make a game spinner, a child folds a six-inch, white construction paper circle in half and then in half again. She unfolds the circle and uses one or more of the following colors to color the four sections: red, blue, yellow, green. Emphasize that it is not necessary to use all four colors. Then she threads a brad through the opening of a paper clip and loosely fastens the brad in the center of the circle so that the paper clip spins freely.

Divide students into four teams and assign each team a different color (making sure that each group member has the color on her spinner). Challenge each team to predict which team member will be first to spin the assigned color ten times. Have each team share its prediction with the class and the reasoning behind it. Next, ask each child to list on provided paper the colors on her spinner. Repeatedly announce, "Spin. [pause] Record." Following your lead, each child spins her spinner and then records on her paper the color on which it stopped. Continue in this manner until one or more teams has a winner. Ask each group to report its findings to the class. If time permits, assign new team colors and play the game again!

Ring Toss

This probability game for partners is sure to ring a bell with students! To prepare, partially fill each of 16 empty plastic soda bottles with water and tightly twist a cap on each one. Press a dot sticker on each cap. Use seven blue stickers, five red stickers, three green stickers, and one yellow sticker. Arrange the bottles on the floor in four rows of four bottles each, leaving plenty of space between the bottles. Provide two eight-inch wooden embroidery hoops for rings. Also provide pencils and copies of "Ring Toss" from page 89. Then use masking tape to mark a toss line.

To begin, each partner writes on her paper the chances of ringing each color and then predicts which color she will ring most often. Next, each partner tosses a ring. If she rings a bottle, she records it on her sheet. Then the students retrieve the rings and toss them again. The partners continue in this manner until they each have ten rings recorded. Then each child uses her data to complete the activity. Later, invite students to share with the class what they learned.

To further extend your students' learning, remove one or more rows of bottles and have students repeat the activity. This time when the students gather to discuss their results, challenge them to explain how the two games of ring toss were different.

Number of letters in name	students
2	||
3	|||
4	|||
5	⧄||| |||
6	||
7	|
8	|
more	|

The Duck Pond

How can a trip to the duck pond be an exercise in probability? Read on! Give each child a clean half-pint milk carton that has the top removed and a yellow construction paper copy of the duck pattern on page 88. A student inverts the carton and writes in permanent marker the number of letters in her first name. Then she cuts out the pattern and glues it to one side of the carton, about one-half inch from the bottom edge. Explain that for this probability game the class predicts which duck number will be plucked most frequently from a pond of water, and then the class tests its prediction. Extract from students that to calculate the odds of this exercise, they must know the total number of ducks, the numbers on the ducks, and how many times each number appears. Create a graph like the one shown to gather the needed information. Then have the class make a prediction based on the data.

Next, place the ducks in a small plastic wading pool that is partially filled with water. Have each child, in turn, pluck one duck from the pond, write its number on a provided tally sheet, and then return the duck to the pond. Use a dowel or similar device to keep the duck pond in constant motion. In conclusion, have students analyze the collected data and discuss the outcome of the activity. Quack!

Button Bonanza

Button, button, which button will it be? For this probability activity students investigate the likelihood of two independent events occurring simultaneously! Show students a two-hole button and a four-hole button and then place ten of each button type in a paper lunch sack. To demonstrate the activity, roll a die and randomly draw one button from the bag. Before you reveal the results of your trial, challenge students to identify the combinations that are possible. Guide them to conclude that you could draw a two-hole button and roll the number 1, 2, 3, 4, 5, or 6. Or you could draw a four-hole button and roll the number 1, 2, 3, 4, 5, or 6. Then, on the chalkboard, write the results of your trial using the format "[2 or 4]-hole button, [number rolled]." Ask students whether they think it is *certain, probable, not probable,* or *impossible* that in 20 trials this combination will occur again. Encourage plenty of discussion.

Place the bag of buttons, a die, pencils, and a recording sheet in a probability game booth (center). Each child visits the booth and records 20 trials on his paper. When every student has completed the activity, find out how many times the combination you demonstrated occurred. Help students understand that the probability of two random events occurring at the same time is less likely than the probability of one random event occurring. In addition, the probability of three random events occurring at the same time is even less likely!

A Sweet Finale

Bring your probability carnival to a close with a delicious assessment activity. Bake a class set of cupcakes. Press an M&M's candy in the top of each baked cupcake, making sure only one orange candy is used. Then apply icing.

Explain that each cupcake has an M&M's candy hidden beneath the icing, but only one cupcake has an orange candy. Ask each child to write on paper his chance of receiving the orange candy *(1 in [number of students in the class])* and how probable it is *(not probable)*. Then collect the papers and hand out the cupcakes. Have each child carefully lick away the frosting from the center of his cupcake to find the candy hidden there before he eats the baked treat!

Name _____   Probability

Go Fish!

There are 20 fish in the pond.
Write how many fish are each color.
_____ are green.   _____ are yellow.
_____ are blue.   _____ are red.

What color fish do you think you will catch most often? _____

Go fish! Write the color of fish you catch each time.

1. _____	6. _____	11. _____	16. _____
2. _____	7. _____	12. _____	17. _____
3. _____	8. _____	13. _____	18. _____
4. _____	9. _____	14. _____	19. _____
5. _____	10. _____	15. _____	20. _____

How many of each color fish did you catch?
_____ green   _____ yellow
_____ blue   _____ red

What color fish did you catch most often? _____

Use the pattern with "The Duck Pond" on page 86.

Ring Toss

There are 16 bottles.
How many bottles have each color cap?
_____ have blue caps.   _____ have green caps.
_____ have red caps.   _____ have yellow caps.

What are the chances you will ring each color of cap?
_____ chance(s) in _____ I will ring a blue cap
_____ chance(s) in _____ I will ring a red cap
_____ chance(s) in _____ I will ring a green cap
_____ chance(s) in _____ I will ring a yellow cap

What color of cap do you think you will ring most often? _____

Toss the ring!

If you ring a bottle, write the color of its cap on the line.
If you do not ring a bottle, write nothing.
Keep tossing until you record ten rings.

1. _____   2. _____   3. _____   4. _____   5. _____

6. _____   7. _____   8. _____   9. _____   10. _____

Show your data on the graph below.

blue										
red										
green										
yellow										
	1	2	3	4	5	6	7	8	9	10

Does your data support your prediction? _____

Explain your answer. _____

_____

_____

UNLOCKING PROBLEM-SOLVING SKILLS

Use this combination of strategy-based activities to unlock your youngsters' problem-solving skills!

ideas by Denine T. Carter

Think Twice!

Logical reasoning is key to a partner game called Think Twice. Each twosome needs a set of 11 dried beans, pennies, or other desired tokens. To play, partners take turns removing one, two, or three tokens from the set. The winner is the player who forces his partner to take the last token. Allow time for each pair to play several games; then invite students to share with the class their strategies for winning. Next, have each child play a few more games with a new partner. No doubt students will think twice before they choose their tokens!

I take three beans and then SHE takes two beans and then... Wait! I take one bean and then...

Delivery Dilemma

When students apply the **guess-and-check** strategy, the solution to this delivery dilemma is no problem! Divide students into small groups and give each group six large paper plates, nine small paper plates, and five blank cards. Explain that you were given 15 pepperoni pizzas to deliver to five teachers; however, you know only the amount that each teacher paid for her order. On the board write the names of five teachers. Beside each name write one of the following amounts: $4.00, $7.00, $10.00, $11.00, $16.00. Instruct each group to label one card per teacher. Also have each group color its plates to resemble pizzas and then label each large pizza "$5.00" and each small pizza "$2.00."

To determine which pizzas the teachers ordered, each group arranges its cards in a column and places a predicted number of pizzas beside each teacher's name. Next, the group calculates the cost of each order and compares it with the amount paid. The group continues in this manner, revising and rechecking its guesses until the dilemma is solved.

For independent practice (or assessment), write the following amounts on the board: $2.00, $6.00, $9.00, $14.00, $17.00. A student copies the amounts on his paper and assigns a different teacher's name to each one. Then, by drawing large and small circles to represent the two pizza sizes, he works independently to determine each teacher's order. Now, that's a challenge that really delivers!

Mrs. Huber $4.00	$2.00 $2.00
Mr. Womack $7.00	$5.00 $2.00
Ms. Reed $10.00	$5.00 $5.00
Ms. Shoaf $11.00	$5.00 $2.00 $2.00 $2.00
Mrs. Vandez $16.00	$5.00 $5.00 $2.00 $2.00 $2.00

Hidden Change

Here's another opportunity for students to cash in on the **guess-and-check** strategy. Ask each child to bring from home a personalized envelope that contains two quarters, five dimes, ten nickels, and ten pennies. (Prepare extra envelopes for students who may need them.) For a review of coin counting, read aloud *The Penny Pot* by Stuart J. Murphy. Then pair students and give each twosome a paper cup and a sheet of paper. To play, Partner 1 removes coins from his envelope that total no more than 50¢ and hides them under the cup. He writes the total value of the hidden coins on the paper and then draws one line for each coin (see illustration). To determine which coins are hidden, Partner 2 manipulates her set of coins on the lines until she finds the combination that equals the written total. After Partner 1 confirms his partner's coin choices, both players return their coins to their envelopes. Then they switch roles and play the game again. For an added challenge, have students hide coins totaling no more than $1.00. What a rich way to boost money and problem-solving skills!

Solution Speedway

The **act-it-out** strategy puts students on the fast track to the results of a car race! Post a laminated chart like the one shown and use a wipe-off marker to program the code with six different colors. Give each student a copy of the race cars from page 92 and a 12" x 18" sheet of drawing paper. Ask each child to color one car for each color listed in the code and then cut out the cars. Next, have her draw on her paper a stretch of racetrack that features a finish line at the far left.

To learn the outcome of each car, fill in each clue on the chart, read it aloud, and allow time for students to arrange their cars on their tracks accordingly. Continue in this manner until the last clue is read. Encourage students to check their work against the completed chart. Then ask a volunteer to share her race results.

To create a new problem for solving, wipe the programming from the chart, list the same six colors in the code in a different order, and repeat the activity. Vroom!

Fashion Flip Book

Students will flip for an activity that requires an **organized list**! Give each child a copy of page 93 and a 6" x 9" piece of construction paper. Use the provided instructions to guide each child in making a fashion flip book. Then have her use her book to determine the number of possible outfits. To do this in an organized manner, she first identifies the different outfits that can be worn with the red hat and then lists her findings on her recording sheet. She repeats the process with the purple hat. Finally, she writes in the small box how many outfits she has made in all and then completes the Bonus Box. Now, that's an activity that will never go out of style!

Steps to make a fashion flip book:
1. Color one hat red and one hat purple.
2. Color one shirt yellow and one shirt orange.
3. Color one pair of shorts blue and the other pair green.
4. Cut along the dotted line. Set the recording sheet aside.
5. Cut along the bold lines. Stack and align the pages.
6. Fold the construction paper in half, tuck the pages inside, staple near the fold, and then decorate the booklet cover as desired.

Candy Combinations

Try this tasty approach to making an **organized list**. Give each child a napkin and a snack-size resealable plastic bag that contains five M&M's candies in each of the following colors: yellow, orange, brown, red, and green. Ask each student to place one candy of each color at the top of her unfolded napkin. Next, direct her to combine the first color with each of the other four colors and place each resulting pair in a column below the single candy as shown. Ask her to repeat this step with each of the remaining colors without forming any duplicate pairs. Then, using a single letter abbreviation for each color, she writes on her math paper the organized list that she's created! *(There are ten possible combinations.)* Confirm each child's work and discuss with the class any patterns that are noticed (such as each column's containing one less pair of candies than the previous column). Then invite each youngster to eat a few candies as she bags her manipulatives for transport home. Delicious!

Patterns

Use the race cars with "Solution Speedway" on page 91.

Name_____

Colorful Clothing

For each color of hat, list the outfits that can be made.
Use the key.

Hat	Shirt	Shorts
R		
R		
R		
R		
P		
P		
P		
P		

Key

R = red
P = purple
Y = yellow
O = orange
B = blue
G = green

How many outfits did you
make in all?

Bonus Box: How many more outfits could be made if there were also a brown hat? Write your answer on the back of this paper and explain it.

©The Education Center, Inc. • *The Best of* The Mailbox® *Math* • *Book 2* • TEC1491

©The Education Center, Inc.

©The Education Center, Inc. • *The Best of* The Mailbox® *Math* • *Book 2* • TEC1491

Note to the teacher: Use with "Fashion Flip Book" on page 91.

Monkeying Around With

Math and Literature

There's no monkey business in this unit—just practical, literature-related ideas for making math meaningful...and FUN!

ideas contributed by Judy Johnson, Lisa Kelly, Sharon Murphy, and Sr. M. Francesca Santacroce

The Greedy Triangle

Written by Marilyn Burns & Illustrated by Gordon Silveria

The greedy triangle loves being busy! Each day it supports bridges, makes music, holds up roofs, and much, much more. For most shapes this lifestyle would be fulfilling. But not for the greedy triangle. Always eager to try new things, the triangle decides it is time to add another line and angle to its shape. Unfortunately this new shape isn't a perfect fit either. Thus begins a succession of new shapes until the greedy triangle no longer knows which side is up!

Use the greedy triangle's shapely experiences to shape up your students' geometry skills! After a just-for-fun oral reading of the story, revisit the book to help students remember what the triangle does as a three-sided shape. List these activities on the chalkboard. Also ask students to suggest other things a triangle could do, and add them to the list. Repeat this activity for each shape that the triangle becomes. Then reveal that the students will be making a mural of a geometry kingdom that is similar to the greedy triangle's home. To do this, each student chooses a different shape and activity from the lists on the chalkboard. Using provided supplies—such as a shape template, construction paper, glue, and markers—the student creates the shape he chose engaged in the activity he chose. Showcase the students' projects on a paper-covered bulletin board titled "Welcome to Shapesville!" Now, that's a king-size way to size up shapes!

12 Ways to Get to 11

Written by Eve Merriam & Illustrated by Bernie Karlin

When this innovative picture book begins, all the numerals from 1 through 12 are present and accounted for—except 11. Where did it go? Is it hiding? Could it be wearing a disguise? The search for the elusive 11 takes the reader to 12 scenes that each feature a different combination of items. And guess what? The items in each scene add up to 11!

So what are the 12 ways to get to 11? To find out have each student number his paper from 1 to 12; then read the story aloud a second time. Stop after each number combination is presented and have the students write the corresponding addition sentence on their papers. Before you proceed, have the class read in unison the sentence that they wrote. After all 12 combinations have been written and read, challenge the class to create other addition sentences that equal 11. Write each combination on the board, and ask each student to number and copy the sentence on his paper. Continue in this manner until the total number of addition sentences on each student's paper equals the class enrollment. Then have every student copy a different sentence from his list onto a large sheet of drawing paper and illustrate it. Challenge older students to write descriptive sentences about their illustrations too. Invite each student to share his work with the class; then bind the projects between two construction paper covers. Accurately title the book (for example, "23 Ways to Get to 11"); then place it in your classroom library for further reading enjoyment.

In the jungle are 10 bananas and 1 very happy monkey.

Pigs Will Be Pigs

Written by Amy Axelrod & Illustrated by Sharon McGinley-Nally

The Pig family has a problem. There's no food in the house, the family is temporarily out of cash, and everyone is hungry! Mrs. Pig knows just what to do! It's time to search the house—from top to bottom—for loose change and forgotten bills. Luckily for the pigs, there's plenty of money to be found, and before long the family is pigging out in a favorite restaurant.

Students will go hog-wild adding up the cash the Pig family finds! For this large-group activity, place a shoebox of transparent coin and dollar-bill cutouts near your overhead projector. You will need a cutout for each of the following coins and bills: penny, nickel, dime, quarter, half-dollar, $1, $2, $5, $10, $20. Then, during a second oral reading of the story, stop after Mr. Pig finds his lucky two-dollar bill. Ask a student volunteer to display the appropriate money cutout on the overhead projector; then write the amount near the top of the screen and return the cutout to the box. Continue your oral reading. Every time money is found, stop and ask a different volunteer to display on the overhead each type of coin or bill that was collected. Then, with input from your students, determine how much money was discovered and add the amount(s) to what has been collected so far. Students will discover that the Pigs have a whopping $34.67 when they leave for the restaurant!

To continue the fun, give each child a copy of the order ticket on page 99 and a copy of a menu from a local restaurant or a menu that you created. Challenge each student to use the menu and his estimation skills to write a dinner order for the pig family that costs no more than $34.67. Next, have each child use a calculator to tally his ticket. Then take a class count to find out how many students stayed within the spending budget. Repeat the activity as many times as desired, providing student copies of the order ticket each time. Order up!

Pigs on a Blanket

Written by Amy Axelrod & Illustrated by Sharon McGinley-Nally

The Pig family is back again, and this time it's looking for a change of pace. At 11:30 the pigs decide a day at the beach is the perfect remedy. After all, the beach is only an hour away, and they can be ready to hit the road in a manner of minutes—or so they think! Delays at home, delays on the road, and delays at the beach impede the pigs. And when the family is finally ready to swim, it's 5:30 and the beach is closing. My, how time flies!

Oink! Oink! Provide loads of hands-on time-telling practice with these precious piggy timepieces! To make a clock like the one shown, a student paints a flattened paper plate pink. After the plate dries, she uses colorful paper, markers or crayons, a brad, precut hour and minute hands, glue, and scissors to create an animated clock face that resembles a pig. To use the clocks, read the story aloud a second time and have each youngster manipulate the hands on her clock to coincide with the piggies' activities. For even more fun, invite each student to tell a story about a real or an imaginary family trip that includes several time-related references. As each student tells her story, have her classmates manipulate the hands on their clocks to coincide with the story events. Time sure flies when you're having fun!

Each Orange Had 8 Slices: A Counting Book

Written by Paul Giganti Jr. & Illustrated by Donald Crews

From ducks to oranges, this brightly illustrated counting book features a series of number-related scenarios that are each accompanied by three related questions.

This story provides the perfect opportunity for students to practice their counting and problem-solving skills. As you read the book aloud, stop after each set of three questions so students can study the picture. Next, reread each question and enlist your students' help in answering it. After the final problem has been solved, have students make a class version of the book.

To begin, a child chooses a place that he likes to visit and imagines several things that he might see on his way there. Then he writes a description of what he sees on a 12" x 18" sheet of drawing paper. Ask each child to begin his writing with the phrase "On my way to…" Next, the youngster carefully illustrates his description and writes three questions about it. Lastly, he turns his paper over and on the back answers each question. Bind the students' work into a classroom volume titled "On My Way to…." Then display the book and challenge students to solve the problems!

A Fair Bear Share

Written by Stuart J. Murphy & Illustrated by John Speirs

Mama Bear promises to make her special blueberry pie if her four cubs gather the nuts, berries, and seeds that she needs. The cubs gather one ingredient at a time and bring it home to count. Mama Bear teaches the cubs to count quickly by putting each ingredient into piles of tens and ones, and she shows them how to regroup a ones pile into a ten. One little cub has another lesson to learn too—there'll be no pie unless each cub does its "fair bear share" of gathering ingredients.

You can count on your students doing their fair share of work in this small-group activity! For every group of four students, program a card with three numbers that have a sum of less than 100. (Do not write the sum on the card.) Appoint a recorder in each group, and give this student the programmed card, a pencil, and paper. Give a paper plate to each remaining group member. In the center of each group, place a container of 99 unshelled peanuts or sunflower seeds, or purple jelly-bean berries.

To begin the activity, the recorder assigns each group member one number from the card. Then, using the cubs' counting strategy, these students count out their assigned number of ingredients onto their paper plates. To find the total number of ingredients collected, two group members combine their ingredients, regrouping if necessary. The recorder draws a picture or writes a number sentence on her paper to document this step. Then the third student adds her ingredients to the collection. The recorder documents this step as well, arriving at the total number of ingredients the group gathered. Check each group's work; then collect the cards and redistribute them to different groups and new group recorders. Repeat the activity. Continue in this manner until each student has been a recorder. Conclude the activity by serving each youngster a "fair share" of a blueberry treat!

Right this way, please.

Dinner at the Panda Palace

Written by Stephanie Calmenson & Illustrated by Nadine Bernard Westcott

It's a very busy night at Panda Palace restaurant, and Mr. Panda, the owner, must find seating for several hungry animals. Whether it's one hungry elephant, two carsick lions, or three pigs running from a wolf, Mr. Panda finds room for them all!

To set the stage for a place-value activity, make a minor adjustment during your first oral reading of the story. Rather than revealing the total number of patrons Mr. Panda seats and serves, replace the story line "Feeding fifty-five diners was no easy task" with the line "Feeding this many diners was no easy task." Then, at the conclusion of the story, ask students how many animals Mr. Panda fed. After a bit of discussion, tell students that you have an idea. Explain that if Mr. Panda seats his patrons at tables for ten, he can easily count his customers. Draw six large circles on the chalkboard and read the story aloud a second time. Stop reading after the first patron, the elephant, enters the restaurant. Ask a student volunteer to mark an X beside one circle to indicate that the elephant has been seated. Continue in this manner until all of Mr. Panda's customers are seated. Then have the students tally the tens and ones to determine the total number of animals Mr. Panda served. Older students can complete a similar seating arrangement on paper.

Give Me Half!

Written by Stuart J. Murphy & Illustrated by G. Brian Karas

There's a typical sibling situation unfolding in this simple rhyming story. A brother and a sister have different ideas about how to split a pizza for lunch. They can't agree on dessert portions either. Or on how much beverage each should get. For a third party, who most likely is a parent, the picture is clear—split everything in half!

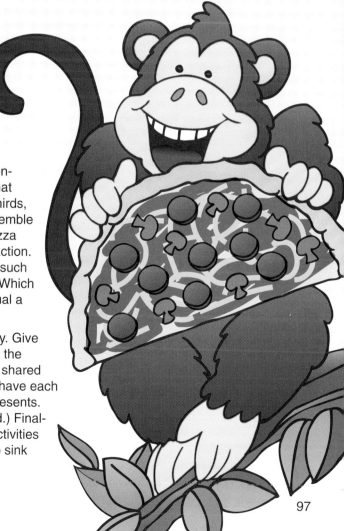

Here's a fraction activity with plenty of taste appeal! At the conclusion of the book, give each student three eight-inch circles that you have visually divided as follows: one into halves, one into thirds, and one into fourths. A student decorates all three circles to resemble her favorite kind of pizza. Then, one at a time, she cuts each pizza apart and labels the backs of the pieces with the appropriate fraction. Next, have students use their pizza slices to answer questions, such as the following: What is the smallest piece of pizza you have? Which is more: one-half or one-third of a pizza? How many fourths equal a half?

Provide additional fraction practice with this appetizing activity. Give each youngster 12 candy pieces in a variety of colors. First, ask the students how many candy pieces they would get to keep if they shared their candy with one friend (or two, three, or four friends). Then have each child determine what fractional part of his candy each color represents. (For example, if five candies are red, then $\frac{5}{12}$ of the candy is red.) Finally, have students eat a portion of their candies and repeat the activities using their new sets. Now, that's an idea students will be glad to sink their teeth into!

Twelve Snails to One Lizard: A Tale of Mischief and Measurement
Written by Susan Hightower & Illustrated by Matt Novak

Milo the beaver needs a branch to patch a hole in his dam. The problem is he can't figure out exactly how long the branch needs to be. His buddy Bubba Bullfrog is full of measurement ideas—from one-inch snails to foot-long lizards to a boa that measures exactly one yard. These pond-side residents might (or might not!) be the perfect measurement tools for getting the job done.

Students will inch their way to better measurement skills with this partner activity! For each student pair, duplicate 12 snail patterns onto brown construction paper and three lizard head and body patterns onto green construction paper (see the patterns on page 99). Have the partners cut out their patterns and glue each lizard head to a lizard body. Also have each twosome decorate a one-yard length of adding-machine tape to resemble a boa.

To begin the activity, write the titles "Snail," "Lizard," and "Snake" on the chalkboard. Then, under your students' direction, list classroom items under each title that could be measured using the corresponding nonstandard unit. Next, have each student pair write one or two items from each list on a sheet of paper, measure each item, and write its measurement beside its name. To conclude the activity, invite students to share the measurements they gathered for the items listed on the chalkboard. Students will quickly see how well they measure up!

How long?		
Student	all day	half day
Milo	X	
Percy	X	
Sally	X	
Jack	X	

The Best Vacation Ever
Written by Stuart J. Murphy & Illustrated by Nadine Bernard Westcott

It's time for a family vacation, and this busy family can't even find the time to decide where to go. Should the place be warm or cool? Near or far? Exciting or relaxing? It's the youngest family member who decides to collect a little data and determine the perfect vacation spot for her active family!

It will probably take only one oral reading of this delightful picture book and your youngsters will be ready to plan their own family vacations! Instead suggest that the students use the method described to plan a special classroom event. To begin, ask students to brainstorm a variety of questions that will help them determine what type of special event to plan. Questions might include the following: Should the event be inside or outside? Should the event be related to math, reading, social studies, or science? Should students dress up for the event? Next, design a simple chart that can be used to collect data for each question. Rather than listing every child's name on each chart, make it each child's responsibility to sign and indicate his answer on every chart. Then post the charts in an area that is easily accessible, and make available a variety of colorful markers for students to use to record their answers. When each child has had an opportunity to contribute to each chart, enlist your students' help in calculating and recording the total number of responses for each answer. Then help the students use the information they've gathered to plan a special classroom event. Let the fun begin!

Use the lizard patterns with *Twelve Snails to One Lizard* on page 98.

Glue.

Use the order ticket with *Pigs Will Be Pigs* on page 95.

Order Up!

Item	Price
	.
	.
	.
	.
	.
	.
	.
	.
	.
Total	$ ___ . ___

Use the snail patterns with *Twelve Snails to One Lizard* on page 98.

Shel Silverstein's outrageous poems add up to countless opportunities for teaching math-related skills! Watch the enthusiasm of your youngsters multiply as they giggle their way through the following poems and math activities. The only way to sum it up is *total* fun!

ideas by Lisa Leonardi

A Light in the Attic
The poems reviewed on pages 100 and 101—"Snake Problem," "Overdues," and "Homework Machine"—are from *A Light in the Attic* by Shel Silverstein.

"Snake Problem"
What do you do when a 24-foot python says, "I love you"? That's the lengthy dilemma facing the child in this love poem.

A 24-foot python is the perfect tool to help your students inch their way toward better measurement skills! After several oral readings of the poem, have each student draw and color a snake on a provided card and then write his name on the card for easy identification. Before asking students to estimate the distance of 24 feet, show them a one-foot paper snake (or a ruler) as a frame of reference. Then lead students into the hallway. On a wall designate the end of an imaginary 24-foot python. Instruct each student to tape his snake card to the wall where he thinks the python's head would be if the snake stretched out to its full 24-foot length. To check the accuracy of your students' estimates, tape a 24-foot length of yarn along the wall. Wow! What a snake!

Students will slither their way to better nonstandard measurement skills with this partner activity! Give each pair of students a one-foot construction paper python, a pencil, paper, and a variety of manipulatives such as Unifix cubes, paper clips, craft sticks, and cotton swabs. Have partners measure the length of their python using each type of manipulative and record their findings on the paper as shown. To conclude the activity, have student pairs compare their findings. For older students, multiply the fun by asking them to calculate the number of manipulatives needed to create snakes of various lengths. For example, "If ten small paper clips are needed to make a one-foot python, how many paper clips are needed to make a five-foot snake?"

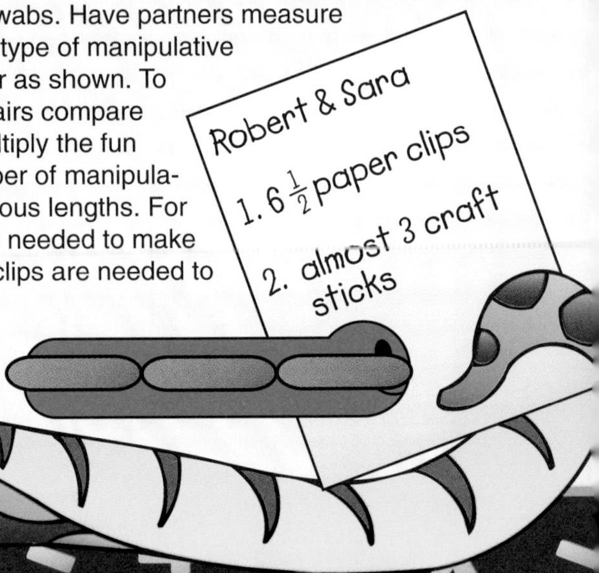

Robert & Sara
1. $6\frac{1}{2}$ paper clips
2. almost 3 craft sticks

"Homework Machine"

The Homework Machine would be the most perfect contraption if only nine plus four equaled three!

Students will be eager to teach this homework machine a thing or two about basic math facts! Copy the poem on chart paper and display it in a prominent classroom location. As you read the poem aloud, have students follow along or read aloud with you. Then enlist your students' help in fixing the homework machine! To begin the repair, tape a blank card over the word *not* (in the next-to-last line of the poem) so that instead of being a not-so-perfect homework contraption, it becomes a perfect one! Also tape a laminated card over each of the two sums, and a laminated sentence strip (or something similar) over the math fact. Next, use a wipe-off marker to program each laminated card with the same sum. Challenge students to write on their papers addition sentences that equal the posted sum. After several minutes, invite the students to share the sentences they created. Be sure to try out a few of the sentences in the poem. To do this, use your wipe-off marker to program the sentence strip with the desired number sentence. After the poem has been recited, wipe away the number sentence and the strip is ready to reprogram for another oral reading.

For a daily kid-pleasing math challenge, keep the poem on display. Each day, reprogram the two laminated cards with a desired numeral and challenge students to write a designated number of math sentences (addition, subtraction, and/or multiplication) that equal the posted numeral. This homework machine works like a charm!

"Overdues"

A library book is found that is long overdue—42 years, to be exact! The question remains whether to return the book or hide it again.

After a few oral readings of "Overdues," this book-related activity is sure to make "cents" at your math center! Check out several books from your school library. Insert an overdue notice with a different fine inside the pocket of each library book. Place the books and a large supply of plastic or paper coins at a center. A student selects a book and uses the coins to pay the fine. Either check students' work or provide a self-checking answer key that lists the possible coin combinations for each fine.

Further challenge students with this large-group activity. Assign a fine, such as five cents, for each day a book is late. Then, using a variety of books, announce a number of days that each book is overdue. Students calculate each book's fine on their papers. Vary the daily fine and the number of overdue days until your youngsters have "fine-ly" paid their dues!

Where the Sidewalk Ends

The poems reviewed on this page—"Smart," "The Googies Are Coming," and "Band-Aids"—are from *Where the Sidewalk Ends* by Shel Silverstein.

"Smart"

Through a series of trades, a boy takes pride in the fact that after starting off with only a single dollar bill, he ends up with five pennies. And five is more than one, isn't it?

This poem provides the perfect opportunity to teach youngsters that more can be less when it comes to coins! Project a transparency like the one shown from an overhead projector. During a second reading of the poem, stop after the first stanza and have a student volunteer place transparent coins on the overhead to show the boy's first money trade. Then enlist the class's help in determining the amount of money lost during the transaction and record this amount in the third column. Repeat this activity after the second, third, and fourth stanzas. After reading the fifth and final stanza, have students calculate the total amount of money the young boy lost. Older students can complete a similar activity on paper. No doubt your students will feel quite *smart* after completing this coin-trading activity!

Money Had	Traded For	Money Lost
		20 ¢

"The Googies Are Coming"

The googies buy children of all different shapes and sizes, and at all different prices. They'll pay 15¢ for dirty ones, 30¢ for clean ones, and only a penny for noisy ones! What a bargain!

Happy Ones = 40 ¢

After several readings of this money-filled poem, post individual sentence strips showing the price of each type of child the googies want to buy. With your students' help, arrange the strips in descending order based on the prices. Then use the resulting list to enhance your students' problem-solving skills. To do this, give each child a construction paper booklet of blank paper. Instruct each child to write her name and the poem title on the front cover and then illustrate what she thinks a googie might look like on the back cover. Each morning, display a word problem based on the posted list and challenge students to solve the problem in their booklets before the end of the school day. Then, before dismissal, set aside time for the students to compare their solutions with their classmates' and make any necessary adjustments. As an added challenge, invite students to submit to you googie-related problems (with answers) for their classmates to solve.

"Band-Aids"

No need to feel sorry for this boy who's bandaged from head to toe! He doesn't have a cut or even a scratch!

This addition activity is just what the doctor ordered! Copy the poem on the chalkboard. To begin, read the poem aloud and have your students determine how many bandages are on the boy's body. Then erase each number word in the poem and replace it with a blank. Have each child use her best penmanship to copy the poem on handwriting paper, inserting a number word from one to five in each blank. Next, ask each student to tally the number of bandages the boy is wearing in her version of the poem and write this number in the lower right-hand corner of her paper. Finally, pair students and have each student check her partner's work. Encourage partners to work together to make any needed corrections. Conclude the activity by attaching a colorful bandage to the back of each child's hand or to her work.

Falling Up

The poems reviewed on this page—"The Monkey" and "Keepin' Count"—are from *Falling Up* by Shel Silverstein.

2 dogs
8
10 bones.

"The Monkey"

1 monkey who visited a banana 3 (tree) on his way 2 the store got a stomachache from 7 green bananas that he 8. Silverstein's clever substitution of numbers for words makes this poem a delight 4 youngsters 2 read!

Students will go bananas as they try to decipher this intriguing poem! Before sharing the poem with your students, copy it onto chart paper. Cover each numeral with a card that you've labeled with a number sentence that equals the concealed numeral. As you read the poem aloud, have students solve each number sentence and supply the missing numeral. Then, for a fun follow-up, have each student use the same style of writing to pen a sentence for a classmate to read. Your youngsters are cer10 2 have a gr8 time!

"Keepin' Count"

A student is determined to find out how many flies are in Professor Bacar's jar. He counts to three million and seven, but when a fly lady has a fly baby, he has to start counting again!

You can count on students going buggy over this estimation activity! Purchase a bag of plastic flies and a few plastic spiders from a party shop or the Oriental Trading Company (1-800-875-8480). Put the flies in a clear jar (with a lid) and display the jar in a prominent classroom location. Also post a recording chart similar to the one shown. After an oral reading of the poem, ask each student to estimate the number of flies in the displayed jar. Record each student's estimate on the chart; then enlist the students' help in counting the flies. Write this number on the chart too. Return the flies to the jar and use a permanent marker to draw a line around the jar that shows where the flies stop. Then drop a few spiders in the jar and secure the lid. Remind students that spiders eat flies!

After the students have left for the day, remove a noticeable amount of flies from the jar. The following school day, have the youngsters repeat the estimating and counting activities. Encourage the students to study the jar and refer to the chart so they can use the information that they previously gathered. Repeat the activities two or three more times—on different days—until all the flies have been removed from the jar. Not only will your students have polished their estimation and counting skills, but they'll also have learned a thing or two about the food chain!

STUDENT	DAY 1 Count: 97 Estimation	DAY 2 Count: 52 Estimation	DAY 3 Count: Estimation
Sam	509	110	
Amy	23	35	
Jose	45	70	
Kim	150	41	
Alex	92	87	

Bright Ideas for Making Math Real!

Sunglasses are not required, but they might be fun! Use this sunny collection of activities to reinforce math skills and shed light on ways math can be useful!

Minutes Playing My Guitar

Data Collected By Stuart Smith

Collecting Cool Info

Create a thirst for data! Read aloud Stuart J. Murphy's *Lemonade for Sale.* In this math-linked literature selection, neighborhood kids use a bar graph to track lemonade sales for five days. At the conclusion of the story, help students name weekday data to collect. Suggestions include minutes spent reading, watching TV, or playing soccer; daily high or low outdoor temperatures; and math problems solved.

To complete a weekday data-collecting activity, each child selects a type of data and titles a copy of page 107 accordingly. He writes his name on the provided line and then numbers the graph to reflect the amount of data he anticipates collecting. (If low numbers are expected, he writes numbers from 1 to 10. For higher data numbers, he writes numbers by tens from 10 to 100.) When the students' data-collecting exercise is complete, ask each child to interpret his results for the class.

For a fun finale, take a lemonade break with students and brainstorm a list of more data-collecting opportunities for summer. If desired, invite interested students to make data-collecting booklets by stapling copies of page 107 between construction paper covers.

Measure, Then Munch

Here's a delicious recipe for reinforcing measurement and problem-solving skills! On a table at the front of the room, organize the items from the provided supply list. Then, on the board, write the recipe for Tricky Trail Mix.

First, have each child title his paper "Trail Mix" and rewrite the recipe to show an exact amount of each ingredient. Next, divide students into four groups. Have the members of each group compare their calculations and solve any inconsistencies in their recipe amounts. When a group has a correct recipe (see Answer Keys on page 160 to verify), it earns a turn at the supply table. Here all group members participate in making a batch of trail mix by measuring ingredients into a provided bag.

When each group has prepared a batch, hand out the paper napkins and invite group members to munch on the mix they made. Prompt students to think of additional opportunities for using their measurement skills.

adapted from an idea by Jill Waldrep—Gr. 3, Sanders Elementary, Austell, GA

Tricky Trail Mix

oat cereal = $\frac{1}{2}$ cup
sunflower kernels = 1 teaspoon
M&M's candies = 3 times the amount of sunflower kernels
raisins = $\frac{1}{2}$ the amount of oat cereal
honey-graham cereal = 3 times the amount of raisins
bite-size pretzels = $\frac{1}{3}$ the amount of honey-graham cereal

Supply List

4 gallon-size resealable plastic bags
measuring cups ($\frac{1}{2}$ c. and $\frac{1}{4}$ c.)
measuring spoon (1 tsp.)
class supply of paper napkins
6 bowls, each containing one of the
  following ingredients:
    4 c. honey-graham cereal
    3 c. oat cereal
    2 c. bite-size pretzels
    2 c. raisins
    $\frac{1}{2}$ c. M&M's candies
    $\frac{1}{4}$ c. sunflower kernels
(A small amount of each ingredient will be left over.)

I had a whole watermelon slice.
I ate ⁵/₈ of it.
How much is left?

There is ³/₈ of the slice left.

Math on the Menu

Provide several delicious servings of computation practice using student-made menus! Give each child three half sheets and two quarter sheets of writing paper. She titles the three half sheets "Breakfast," "Lunch," and "Dinner" and the two quarter sheets "Desserts" and "Drinks." On each paper, she lists three or more of her favorites from the named category and assigns a price to each that falls within a given range. To make her menu, she folds in half a 12" x 18" sheet of construction paper (to 9" x 12"). On the front cover, she writes the name of a personalized eatery and adds desired decorations. She glues the papers she prepared inside. Laminate the menus for durability, if desired.

To complete a menu-related activity, give each child a form like the one shown. Announce a time of day and a spending allowance that includes a count of bills and coins. Use a calculator to check each child's calculations or have students use calculators for this purpose. For added variety, have classmates trade menus before placing their orders. Students are sure to recognize the value of these skills!

Cynthia Mackel—Grs. 1–2

Fair Shares

Pair fractions with food, and students are instantly interested! To begin, have each child fold in half a 9" x 12" sheet of drawing paper and trace a circle or rectangle template on the folded paper. Have him keep his paper folded and cut along the resulting outline. Instruct him to color one shape to resemble a favorite food and then color the second shape to match.

Next, have each child glue one cutout to the top half of a 9" x 12" sheet of light-colored construction paper. Also, give every student a sticky note labeled with a fraction. Below his glued drawing, a child writes a word problem about the food shown that includes the fraction he was given. To solve the problem, he turns his paper over and cuts the remaining shape into equal-size pieces. Then, in a manner similar to the one shown, he glues the pieces on the top half of the paper and circles and writes the answer.

To follow up, challenge students to describe ways in which they benefit from their knowledge of fractions. Perhaps sharing a package of animal crackers will enhance their thinking.

Cynthia Mackel—Grs. 1–2
Rosemont Elementary School
Baltimore, MD

This math game sharpens computation skills and shows students a great way to pass time during a road trip! Two or more can play. Each player needs a notepad and pencil. To begin play, say, "I spy," followed by two numbers, their locations, and a math operation. For example, "I spy a 2 on the board and a 7 on the calendar. Multiply!" The first player to solve the problem says, "Solved!" Ask for this student's answer. If the answer is correct, say, "Correct! Your turn." The winning player then spies the numbers for the next round of play. If the answer is incorrect, say, "Sorry, the answer is 14. Let's play again!" and begin a new round. Play a few rounds. When students are familiar with the game, divide them into small groups and have each group continue play on its own.

When game time is over, challenge students to name places where numbers can be spied during a trip. Answers may include highway signs, mile markers, exit signs, and license plates.

Suggest that students pack pencils and notepads for their next family outing and teach their families how to play this numbers game!

Deborah Cox—Grs. 1–2
Lost River Elementary
Bowling Green, KY

Shop Around

Students are sure to take a shine to this shopping center! Stock a corner of the classroom with clean and nonbreakable food packaging. Label each item with a purchase price. (To create an awareness of the value of money, use realistic prices.) Place a plastic shopping basket and a calculator at the center. Also, post a laminated sign that reads "Today's spending allowance is" and use a wipe-off marker to program the sign with a desired amount of money.

A shopper attempts to load the basket with items that come close to, but do not exceed, the posted amount. To do this, she rounds each purchase price and mentally calculates the total price of the items in the basket. When she is finished shopping, she uses the calculator to find the exact sum of her purchases and to determine whether she met her goal. To increase the difficulty of the center, provide coupons that can be used on select items.

Encourage students who accompany their parents on shopping trips to ring up estimation and mental math skills all summer long!

Wendy Borsari and Jennifer Steinman—Gr. 3
Hillcrest Heights Elementary
Prince George's County, MD

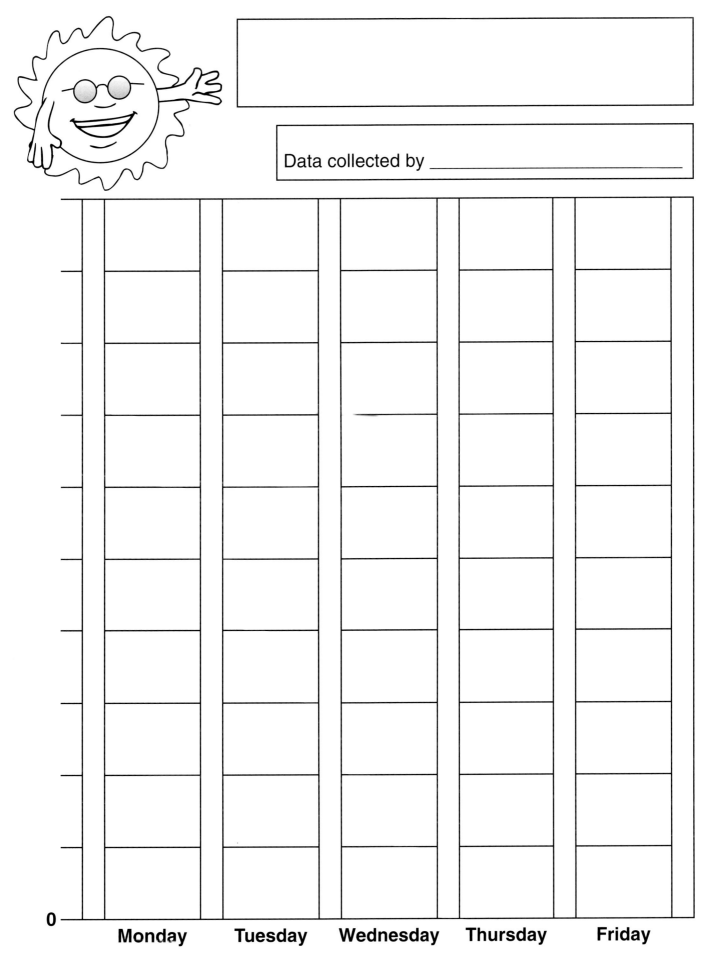

Data collected by _____

0 — **Monday**   **Tuesday**   **Wednesday**   **Thursday**   **Friday**

Note to the teacher: Use with "Collecting Cool Info" on page 104.

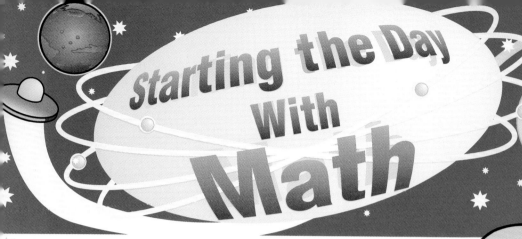

Starting the Day With Math

A hearty helping of math each morning is top-notch nourishment for thinking skills. Plus it's just an out-of-this-world way to start every day! Pick and choose from the following easy-to-implement ideas!

Money Matters

Cash in on money skills with these calendar-related activities!

- Have students brainstorm coin combinations that equal the current date. For example, for September 20, possible combinations include two dimes, 20 pennies, one dime and two nickels, and so on.
- At the beginning of each month place one coin in a designated container for each day in that month. Vary the value of the coins. Then, every day, have a student take coins from the container to represent the current date (e.g., two coins on the second, ten coins on the tenth). Lead the class in calculating the cash value of the day and then return the coins to the container.

$$6 - 2 = 4$$

VIRTUAL DICE PROJECTOR

Mental Math

Get each morning rolling with some thought-provoking computation! Near the class calendar, mount three laminated squares, one laminated circle, and an equal sign in the order shown. To begin, have one student roll a die. Use a wipe-off marker to write the number he rolls in the first laminated square. Ask another student to roll the die and write the number he rolls in the third laminated square. Give the class ample time to mentally solve the equation. Then ask a volunteer to name the missing operation and number as you add them to the math sentence. Next, have the volunteer explain for his classmates how he solved the equation. You'll quickly discover that the students' verbal explanations are invaluable for promoting their classmates' problem-solving skills. For a more difficult activity, provide two dice for students to roll and then write the numbers each child rolls as a two-digit number. Roll on!

Trisha Owen—Gr. 3, Libbey Elementary School, Wheatland, WY

Hundreds Board

You can count on this activity to liven up the group. Position a laminated hundreds chart near your class calendar. Each morning, after the calendar is updated, use the chart to load the students in rousing counts—by ones, by twos, by fives, and by tens. For extra fun, vary the beat of the count and add accompanying movements.

Lisa Strieker—Gr. 3
St. Paul Elementary School
Highland, IL

clap
clap
clap

2, 4, 6, 8, 10...

Welcome to Mrs. Squid's Second Grade!

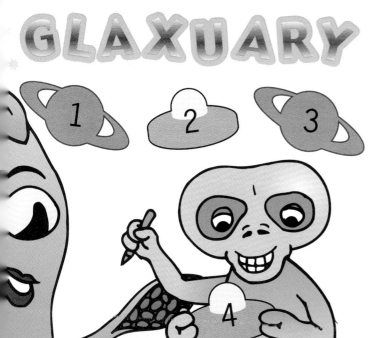

GLAXUARY

Patterning Possibilities

If one picture is worth a thousand words, imagine the chatter your classroom calendar will create when you use it to reinforce patterning skills! Each month, prepare calendar pieces that reveal a different pattern relating to the month, season, or a current theme or topic of study. Keep the pieces in a container near the calendar. At the beginning of the month, ask each child on daily calendar duty to state the current date before finding and posting the corresponding cutout. As soon as the monthly pattern is established, each child on calendar duty states the day's date and identifies the shape and/or color of the corresponding cutout before he adds it to the calendar. Increase the difficulty of the pattern each month, and by the end of the year your youngsters will be pros at identifying patterns!

Sherrie L. Scott
Warnsdorfer School
East Brunswick, NJ

Weather Graph

Collecting, displaying, and discussing weather-related data reinforces a variety of math concepts. Display a bar graph, like the one shown, near your classroom calendar. Each morning, the daily weather reporter graphs the current weather condition and then asks the class two or three graph-related questions. On the last day of each month, remove all the data that's been collected. The outlook for this morning's math activity is sunny and bright!

Lisa Strieker—Gr. 3
St. Paul Elementary School
Highland, IL

Weather conditions indicate moderate cloudiness....

MONTHLY WEATHER DATA

10
9
8
7
6
5

Enticing Estimation

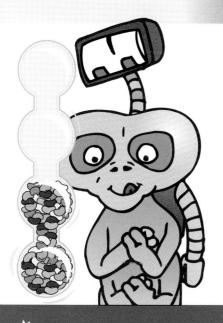

Take a daily approach to estimation and your students' accuracy is sure to increase! Each week, provide a different snack item to be estimated. Before the students arrive on Monday morning, count out several snack items into a clear, airtight container. When a student arrives, she studies the contents of the container and records her estimate in her math journal or at a display provided for this purpose. Later in the day, reveal the exact number of snack items in the container. For each remaining day of the week, add or delete items from the container, always keeping an accurate count, and always revealing this count to the students after their estimates are made. Encourage students to utilize the count(s) from the previous day(s) when making new estimates. Then, on Friday, invite the student with the most accurate estimate to evenly distribute the snack items to her classmates, keeping any remainders for herself. Fine-tuning estimation skills is a very tasty experience!

adapted from an idea by Christine Joyner—Gr. 1, Lincoln Heights GT Magnet School
Fuquay–Varina, NC

Daily Report

Math and spelling skills are reinforced with this six-part morning exercise. On a bulletin board, showcase a classroom calendar; a clock with manipulative hands; a large laminated rectangle; and three small and empty containers labeled "ones," "tens," and "hundreds" for holding craft sticks. Nearby store a set of day-of-the-week cards, calendar pieces for the month, approximately 20 craft sticks, a wipe-off marker, pushpins, and other needed supplies. Every Monday, place a weekly report form like the one shown on each child's desk. Each day as the class is settling in, a different student updates the calendar, posts the appropriate day-of-the-week card, programs the clock with a designated time, increases the daily count by one, and uses the wipe-off marker to copy a provided math problem on the laminated rectangle. Then each child completes morning math by referring to the updated calendar display and recording the information on his weekly form. Establish a timely and efficient method of checking morning math. To keep interest high, periodically announce Four-Star Friday and allow each child who aced morning math every day that week to take Friday off!

Erin Hoffman—Gr. 3, Brecknock Elementary School, Shillington, PA

Nifty Number Board

Spend a few minutes each morning at this number board and students' math, listening, and direction-following skills are sure to prosper! Visually divide a sheet of poster board into 12 equal sections; then laminate the board. Program 12 small cards or seasonal cutouts with different numbers for adding (subtracting, multiplying, or dividing) and use Velcro to attach the cards to the board, one per section. Each morning, point to a card on the number board. Then provide a series of oral directions like, "To find today's morning math number, go two cards up and one card to the right." Instruct each student to write and circle the corresponding number on his math paper (or in his math journal). Confirm the morning math number and then pose math problems for the students to solve that incorporate it—for example, "Find the sum of our morning math number and today's date" or "When counting by twos, what five numbers follow today's morning math number?" Continually update the number board by repositioning or replacing the numbers on it. And today's morning math number is…

Karen Saner—Grs. K–1, Burns Elementary, Burns, KS

MANAGEMENT

A Fair Approach

Making sure that each student is assured equal participation in a variety of morning math and calendar activities can be tricky. A class management sheet like the one shown works well. A quick glance reveals which students have and have not participated in each activity. You'll also have a central place for jotting notes about each youngster's performance. Students are sure to appreciate your fair approach to these highly anticipated morning activities.

Ashley Rebman—Gr. 2, Durham, NC

	Calendar	Clock	Place Value	Weather Chart	Money Chart	Mental Math	Estimation
Cosmo	✓						
Zelto		✓					
Nefton			needed help				
Myopeea			✓				

Hundred-Chart Investigation

Set your young sleuths hot on the trail of intriguing number patterns, mysteries, and challenges with these hundred-chart ideas!

Mystery Number

What does every math sleuth need? A number finder! Give each student a copy of a lens pattern on page 113 and a jumbo craft stick. Have the youngster cut along the outer edge of the pattern and then carefully cut out the inner rectangle (provide assistance as necessary). Instruct him to glue the lens to the craft stick as shown and then sign his name on the resulting handle. To present a case to be solved, give each student a hundred chart. Secretly choose a number between 1 and 100. Use the terms *greater than* and *less than* to identify the numbers immediately preceding and following the chosen number. Challenge students to use the clues and their number finders to locate the mystery number on their charts. Case solved!

adapted from an idea by Karen Saner—Grs. K–1
Burns Elementary
Burns, KS

Spin Off!

Count on students to track down large numbers with this partner game! Provide each twosome with a copy of the spinner on page 113, scissors, a paper clip, a hundred chart, a sheet of paper for keeping score, and a different-colored counter for each player. Have one player cut out the spinner. Explain that the goal of the game is to make the greatest numbers. To begin, one player uses a pencil and the paper clip to spin twice. He combines the numbers he got to make a two-digit number. (If the spinner lands on the star, he uses a number of his choice.) For example, if the spinner lands on 3 and 4, he may make either 34 or 43. The player places his counter in the corresponding square on the hundred chart. The second player takes a turn in a like manner. The player with the greater number earns one point. The players clear the chart. The game continues until one player earns five points and is declared the winner.

Sniff Sniff

Pattern Seekers

There's more to a hundred chart than meets the eye! Tell the class that a hundred chart has several horizontal, vertical, and diagonal patterns. Allow time for students to study a displayed hundred chart; then invite volunteers to share patterns they see. Next, give each student a booklet with construction paper covers and a desired number of pages formatted like the one shown. Instruct her to title the booklet "Detective [student's name]'s Math Notes." Throughout your hundred-chart unit, challenge students to find a variety of patterns. When a youngster discovers a pattern, have her illustrate it on a hundred chart and write about it in the provided space. No doubt students will be eager to share their discoveries, so be sure to provide time for a class debriefing!

1	2	3	4	5	6	7	8	9	10
11	12	13	14	15	16	17	18	19	20
21	22	23	24	25	26	27	28	29	30
31	32	33	34	35	36	37	38	39	40
41	42	43	44	45	46	47	48	49	50
51	52	53	54	55	56	57	58	59	60
61	62	63	64	65	66	67	68	69	70
71	72	73	74	75	76	77	78	79	80
81	82	83	84	85	86	87	88	89	90
91	92	93	94	95	96	97	98	99	100

Found: A diagonal pattern

Evidence: Start with 9. Move down diagonally.

For each number in that line, the digits add up to 9.

Letter-Perfect

Close inspection of a hundred chart reveals not only patterns but letters too! In advance, copy a class supply of hundred charts plus one extra. On one copy, color the appropriate squares to form a selected letter. To begin, give each youngster a copy of an unmarked chart. Announce that you have discovered something special about the chart—a letter is concealed in it! To provide proof of your claim, verbally provide step-by-step directions for finding and marking each square needed to form the letter. For example, a direction for 63 might be the following: "Find 65. Color the number that is two less." If desired, provide additional hundred charts and challenge your youngsters to uncover other letters!

1	2	3	4	5	6	7	8	9	10
11	12	13	14	15	16	17	18	19	20
21	22	23	24	25	26	27	28	29	30
31	32	33	34	35	36	37	38	39	40
41	42	43	44	45	46	47	48	49	50
51	52	53	54	55	56	57	58	59	60
61	62	63	64	65	66	67	68	69	70
71	72	73	74	75	76	77	78	79	80
81	82	83	84	85	86	87	88	89	90
91	92	93	94	95	96	97	98	99	100

If you have 47 and add 12, what do you get?

You get 59!

100th Day Riddles

What better way to celebrate the 100th day of school than with a kid-pleasing hundred-chart activity? Read aloud *100 Days of School* by Trudy Harris, a collection of riddles that explores the concept of 100. Then provide each student with a hundred chart and a half sheet of paper. Secretly assign each student a different number from 1 to 100. Instruct the youngster to refer to the chart as he creates an addition or subtraction riddle about his number. Then have him write the riddle and its answer on his paper. Ask a volunteer to read his riddle aloud without revealing the answer. Then challenge his classmates to use their hundred charts to determine the answer. Invite the first student who correctly answers the riddle to share her riddle next. (If she has already shared it, have her call on another student.) Continue in a like manner until every riddle has been answered.

Missing!

Number sense helps crack this missing numbers case! Display a poster-size 100-box grid. Program each of several grid boxes to begin creating a hundred chart. Cut a copy of a hundred chart into individual number cards. Remove the card for each number written on the grid and then place the cards in a container labeled "Evidence."

Tell students that although most of the numbers on the hundred chart have mysteriously disappeared, you have collected evidence that will help reconstruct the chart. Each day, ask a volunteer to remove a card and read it aloud. Ask her to find the corresponding grid box by counting back, counting forward, continuing a pattern, or using another appropriate strategy of her choice. When she identifies the correct box, have her tell the class her strategy and then write the number in the box. Invite a desired number of additional volunteers to contribute to the chart in a like manner. Repeat the process each day until the chart is complete.

Rosemary Camiolo—Grs. 1–2, Looping
Bells Elementary
Turnersville, NJ

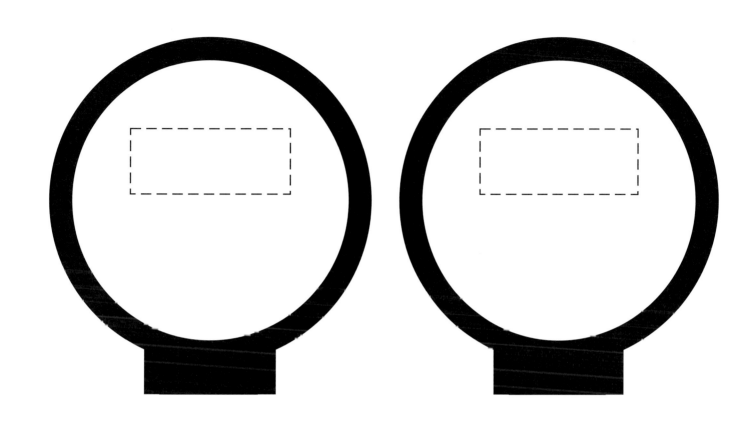

Use the spinner with "Spin Off!" on page 111.

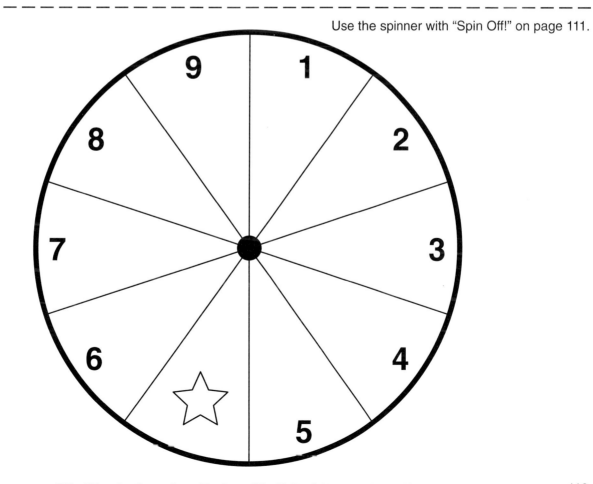

Blue-Ribbon Recipes
for Math Reinforcement

When we asked our trusty subscribers for their favorite math activities, we received a full-course menu of prizewinning suggestions! In this delicious assortment, you'll find ideas for strengthening assorted skills, from basic facts to expanded notation. Serve up these appetizing activities and watch students develop an undeniable taste for math!

On-Target Fact Review

This large-group game is right on target when it comes to re-inforcing basic math facts! Draw a dartboard on the chalkboard. For a review of addition facts, label each section of the dartboard with a different sum. Group students into two teams and have each team stand single file facing the chalkboard. The first player in each line takes a turn choosing a sum from the dartboard and stating a corresponding addition fact. If a correct fact is given, the player scores team points equal to the sum. (To avoid repetition of facts, write the sums on the chalkboard and list each correct fact under its answer.) If an incorrect fact is given, no points are scored. Both players then move to the end of their respective lines. Continue play as described until all students have partici-pated at least once. The team with the most points wins!

Heather Fischer—Gr. 2, Prairie Heights Elementary, Dwight, KS

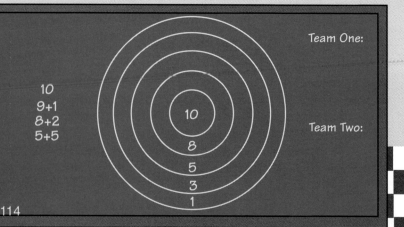

Flash Card Tic-Fact-Toe!

Add a mathematical twist to tic-tac-toe with this large-group game. For a review of subtrac-tion facts, have each child label 15 to 20 con-struction paper cards with provided subtraction facts and write the corresponding answers on the backs. To make her gameboard, a child chooses nine cards from her set and arranges them, fact side up, in three rows of three cards each. To begin play, call the answer to one of the provided subtraction facts. Each child checks her array of cards for a matching subtraction fact. If she finds one, she turns the card over to confirm her selection. If the answer matches, she leaves the answer showing. If it does not, she flips the card over so that the fact shows. (Only one fact card may be turned over for each stated answer.) The first student to show three answers in a vertical, horizontal, or diagonal row on her gameboard declares, "Tic-fact-toe!" As soon as a game winner is confirmed, each child creates a new nine-card gameboard. At the end of game time have each child store her cards in a plastic sandwich bag for future games.

10-7	5	4-2
11-4	8-2	0
9-8	3-0	10-6

Ron Derr—Gr. 3, Brecknock Elementary School Shillington, PA

Addition Facts to 7 by Samantha

0 + 7 = 7   7 + 0 = 7
1 + 6 = 7   6 + 1 = 7
2 + 5 = 7   5 + 2 = 7
3 + 4 = 7   4 + 3 = 7

Buried Treasure

If you're searching for a way to reinforce basic addition facts, you'll find this treasure chest project as precious as gold! Select a sum on which students need extra reinforcement, such as sums to 7. Or for an individualized project, help each child select a sum that she finds especially challenging. Then have each child list and solve basic addition facts that total the spotlighted sum. After verifying the students' work for accuracy, help them make treasure chests in which to record their precious problems. To make a chest, a student folds up the bottom of an 8" x 18" strip of light-colored construction paper to make a seven-inch flap. Next, she folds the top four inches of the strip forward. She rounds the top corners of the folded shape, unfolds the shape, and then copies her problems inside. Instruct each student to refold her shape. If desired, also have her round one end of a 1" x 5" paper strip and glue it to the top flap of the folded shape as shown. Then invite her to title and decorate her resulting treasure chest as desired. Finally, encourage each child to refer to her treasure chest as she works on memorizing the facts that she's stored there.

adapted from an idea by VaReane Gray Heese—Gr. 2, Springfield Elementary Springfield, NE

Odd and Even

Get youngsters in tune with odd and even numbers with the little ditty shown! As soon as students are familiar with the song, try this follow-up activity. Give each child ten animal crackers. Announce a number from one to ten. A student counts out the corresponding number of crackers and groups them by twos to determine if the number is odd or even. If the number is even, she oinks. If the number is odd, she moos! Repeat the activity several times, announcing a different number each time. Then serve milk or juice and invite students to eat their crackers!

Gale Gervais Yost—Gr. 1, Whiting Lane Elementary West Hartford, CT

Odd and Even
(sung to the tune of "B-I-N-G-O")

There was a farmer who had a pig,
And Even was his name-o.
0, 2, 4, 6, 8; 0, 2, 4, 6, 8; 0, 2, 4, 6, 8;
And Even was his name-o.

There was a farmer who had a cow,
And Odd was her name-o.
1, 3, 5, 7, 9; 1, 3, 5, 7, 9; 1, 3, 5, 7, 9;
And Odd was her name-o.

Add It!

You can sum up this partner game in one word—FUN! Each child needs a pencil, a sheet of paper, and a die. For each round of play, a partner rolls his die twice and writes the two numbers he rolls as a two-digit number. Then he makes a second two-digit number in the manner described and uses it to create a two-digit addition problem on his paper. He solves the addition problem and then he asks his partner to check his work. Next, the partners compare sums. The partner with the higher sum scores a point for the round. If the sums are equal, both partners earn a point. Students continue playing in this same mannor until time is called. The partner with the most points at the end of game time wins! Add 'em!

Jodi Moll—Gr. 3, Fairfax Elementary, Valley, AL

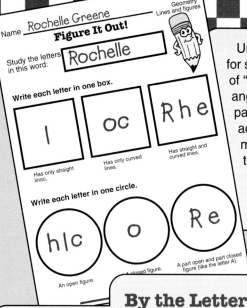

Name Rochelle Greene

Geometry
Lines and figures

Figure It Out!

Study the letters
in this word:

Rochelle

Write each letter in one box.

| l | oc | Rhe |
| Has only straight lines. | Has only curved lines. | Has straight and curved lines. |

Write each letter in one circle.

hlc

o

Re

An open figure.

A closed figure.

A part open and part closed figure (like the letter A).

What's in a Name?

Understanding curved and straight lines and open and closed figures is a cinch for students when they take this personalized approach. Give each student a copy of "Figure It Out!" from page 119. Have each child write his first name in the rectangle at the top of the page and then complete the activity as described. Next, pair students and have each child confirm his partner's answers. To extend the activity, enlist the students' help in identifying the student names that have the most (least) letters in each category presented. Then invite interested students to repeat the activity using their middle names, last names, nicknames, family members' names, pets' names, or other desired word choices.

Shelly Lanier, Reeds Elementary, Lexington, NC

By the Letter

Students take a personal interest in this patterning activity! Have each child continuously write his name from left to right on a sheet of one-inch graph paper—one letter per square—until each square is written in. To make his pattern, he assigns a different color to each letter in his name and then colors the one-inch squares accordingly. Encourage students to study the patterns they make and compare them with the patterns their classmates make. Mount the students' projects on a bulletin board titled "Name Patterns—Unique Just Like Us!"

Diane Wiss—Gr. 2, Fox Meadow School, South Elgin, IL

Searching for Solid Shapes

Send students on a search for solid shapes with this homework activity! Give each child a copy of "Solid Shape Hunt" from page 119. Have him write a search location such as "kitchen" or "bedroom" in the first blank at the top of the page and a due date in the second blank. When the homework papers are returned, compile the students' research on individual solid shape posters and then use the information gathered to create a class graph (see the illustration). Pose a variety of graph-related questions for students to answer. Wow! Solid shapes are everywhere!

Marjorie Crawford, Herndon, VA

Cylinders We Found

soup can	dog food can
potato chip can	cat food can
coffee can	vegetable can
biscuit can	salt container
soda can	oatmeal container
tuna fish can	

Searching the Kitchen for Solid Shapes

Shapes	Items Found											
cube												
box												
cone												
sphere												
cylinder												
	1	2	3	4	5	6	7	8	9	10	11	12

Measure It!

1 2 3 4 5 6 7 8 9 10 11 12

3 inches long by 2 inches wide

How long? How wide?

For Good Measure

Keep students' measurement skills in tip-top shape and create a class book with this fun-to-repeat activity! Have each child copy the two questions "How long?" and "How wide?" near the bottom of a 4½" x 12" rectangle of white construction paper. Next, she draws and colors a picture of a desired item on the remainder of her paper, measures the length and width of the illustrated item at its longest and widest points, and records the resulting measurements on the back of her paper. Ask students to trade their completed papers with another classmate and confirm the measurements written on the back. As students work, decorate two 4½" x 12" rectangles of yellow construction paper to resemble rulers. Then collect the students' work and compile the pages between the resulting yellow covers. Title the book "Measure It!" and place the book and a ruler in your math center. A student measures the length and width of each illustrated item and then turns the page to check her work. Now, that's a project that really measures up!

Leigh Anne Newsom—Gr. 3, Greenbrier Intermediate, Chesapeake, VA

Lunch Money

Create an appetite for money-counting skills with this whole-group activity. Sequentially number a class set of resealable plastic bags, seal a different combination of real coins inside each bag, and prepare a corresponding answer key. Place the bags and answer key in a lunchbox for safekeeping. Prepare a math journal for each child that contains one blank page for each prepared coin set. Give the math journals to the students and have them number the pages. Every morning place a different coin set on each child's desk. A student counts the lunch money without opening the bag. On the corresponding page in his journal, he writes the total money amount and then draws and colors the matching coin set. Collect the bags and store them in the lunchbox. Repeat the activity daily until every student has counted each bag of lunch money. Periodically collect the students' journals and use the answer key to check their work.

Kathie Jamieson—Gr. 1, Fulton Grammar School, Fulton, MS

Got the Time?

This large-group game provides timely feedback on time-telling skills! To make the game cards, use a clock stamp and an ink pad to stamp a clock face on a class supply of blank cards. Program each clock with a different time. If desired, use a red fine-point marker to draw the hour hands and a blue fine-point marker to draw the minute hands. Keep a record of the times shown on the cards. Laminate the cards for durability. To play, distribute the cards and quickly announce each recorded time. The child with the corresponding card holds it up for your approval. When all the times are called, collect the cards, shuffle them, and play another round!

Sandy Shaw
Jeannette McKee Elementary
Jeannette, PA

117

"McMarvelous" Math

Beginning place-value skills are in the bag when you take this kid-pleasing approach! Ask a local fast-food restaurant for a donation of two paper french fry bags per student. Cut 12" x 18" sheets of yellow construction paper into ½" x 5" strips (cut two sheets for every five students) and sequentially number a class supply of paper plates. Give each child a paper plate with a batch of yellow paper fries (no more than 29), two french fry bags, and a sheet of paper. Have each child number his paper to match the paper plate count; then have him bag his fries. Explain that each bag holds ten fries—no more, no less. Any unbaggable fries are to be placed on the paper plate. When his fries are bagged, he writes on his paper (beside the corresponding number) how many fries are in the batch. Then he pours all the fries on the paper plate, and on a signal from you, passes the plate of fries to the next person along a prede-termined route. After bagging several batches of fries, students begin to clearly understand the concept of tens and ones! To increase the difficulty of the activity, have students work in pairs. Give each pair four french fry bags and up to 49 fries to bag. "McMarvelous"!

Patricia Onofrio—Gr. 1, C. T. O'Connell School, Bristol, CT

Stump the Principal

Increase the appeal of word problems with this unique plan. Each child writes three or more word problems for the school principal to solve and then makes a corresponding answer key. Arrange a time for each child to deliver her problems to the principal. The principal solves the problems and returns the paper to the child to grade. The child grades the principal's paper and writes a positive comment on it. Before she returns the paper to the principal, she tells her classmates about her ex-perience and what she plans to tell the principal about his or her work. Word problems will become so appealing that students will be eager to prepare them for family members, friends, and you to solve!

Maria Smith—Gr. 2, Bess Race Elementary, Crowley, TX

Expand It!

These handy manipulatives are ideal for reinforcing expanded form. Cut a supply of sentence strips into one-foot lengths. To make the manipulative shown, write the expanded form of a three-digit number on a one-foot strip. Then fold the strip to reveal the standard form. To do this, reverse-fold the right end of the strip so that the ones digit of the second number is covered. Then make a second reverse fold, this time covering the ones and tens digits of the third number. When folded, the strip shows the standard form of the number. When unfolded, it shows the expanded form. Program your supply of strips with different numbers and place them at a center for students to use. Or have each child contribute one manipulative to the center!

Patti Hirsh—Gr. 3, Casis School, Austin, TX

118

Name _____

Geometry
Solid shapes

Solid Shape Hunt

Search a _____ for _____ solid shapes.
List the items you find in the boxes below.
Return this paper to school by _____.

sphere	cone
cube	box
	cylinder

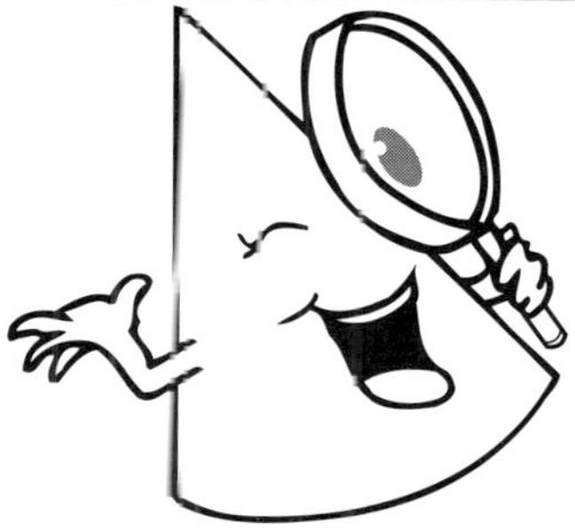

©The Education Center, Inc. • *The Best of The Mailbox® Math • Book 2* • TEC1491

Name _____

Geometry
Lines and figures

Figure It Out!

Study the letters
in this word: ┌─────────┐

Write each letter in one box.

Has only straight
lines.

Has only curved
lines.

Has straight and
curved lines.

Write each letter in one circle.

An open figure.   A closed figure.   A part open and part closed
figure (like the letter A).

©The Education Center, Inc. • *The Best of The Mailbox® Math • Book 2* • TEC1491

Note to the teacher: Use "Figure It Out!" with "What's in a Name?" on page 116. Use "Solid Shape Hunt" with "Searching fo·Solid Shapes" on page 116.

119

A Math Hoedown

Yee-haw! Sashay into full swing with this bumper crop of seasonal math ideas!

Place-Value Monsters

This **place-value game** is monstrously fun for two players! Select the monster cards from page 123 that correspond with your students' place-value skills. Copy the selected cards on white construction paper—one set per child. Have each child color his cards, cut them out, and store them in a resealable plastic bag.

Pair students and give every twosome a die and two half sheets of paper. On his paper, each child draws one blank for each card in his bag. To begin play, announce, "High ([or low]) number." Then each child in turn removes a card from his bag and rolls the die. He writes the number rolled on his paper in the corresponding blank. Play continues in this manner until both players' numbers are made. The child with the higher (or lower) number wins.
Then the cards are returned to the bags, new blanks are drawn, and another round begins!

Kim Fields

Adding With Acorns

Watch your youngsters go nuts over **three-addend addition!** Ask every child to bring ten acorns to school (or provide unshelled peanuts). Give each youngster a resealable plastic bag in which to store her acorns, ten two-inch paper squares to number from 0 to 9, and a small paper cup. Divide students into groups of three and give each trio a box lid and paper. Each player shuffles her number cards and stacks them facedown. One player draws a card from her stack and counts a matching number of acorns into her cup. All players write this addend on their papers. The two remaining players each take a turn as described. To find the sum of the addends, the players pour the acorns from their cups into the box lid, count them, and write the corresponding sum on their papers. Next, each child retrieves her acorns from the box lid, returns them to her plastic bag, and puts the number card she had drawn in a personal discard pile. Then the fun starts again!

Carol A. Horton, Taneytown, MD

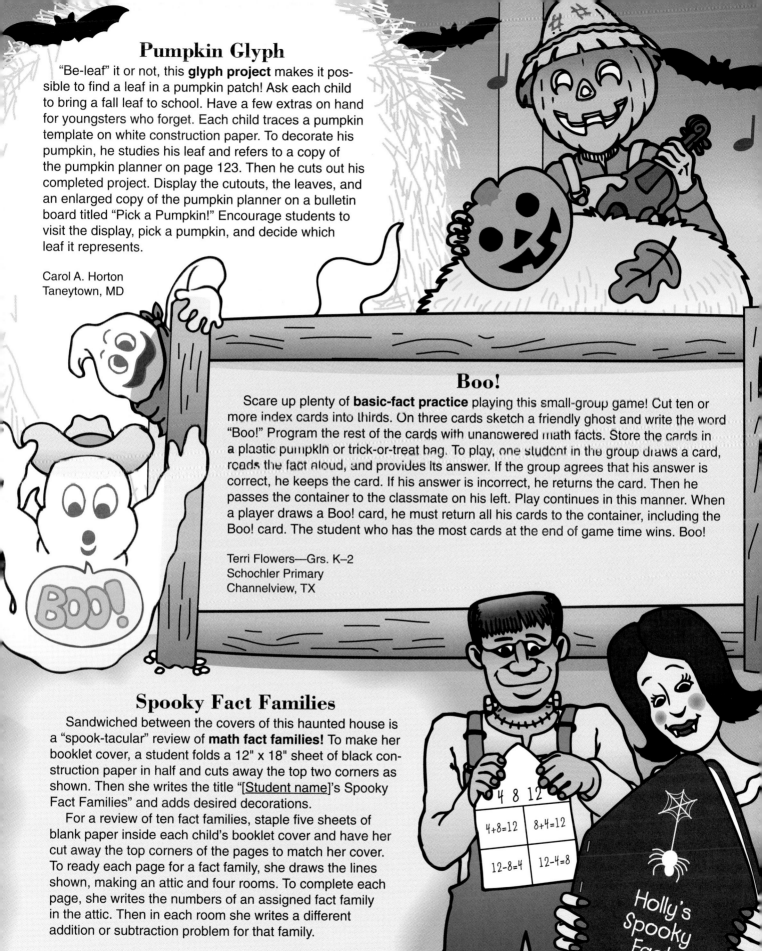

Pumpkin Glyph

"Be-leaf" it or not, this **glyph project** makes it possible to find a leaf in a pumpkin patch! Ask each child to bring a fall leaf to school. Have a few extras on hand for youngsters who forget. Each child traces a pumpkin template on white construction paper. To decorate his pumpkin, he studies his leaf and refers to a copy of the pumpkin planner on page 123. Then he cuts out his completed project. Display the cutouts, the leaves, and an enlarged copy of the pumpkin planner on a bulletin board titled "Pick a Pumpkin!" Encourage students to visit the display, pick a pumpkin, and decide which leaf it represents.

Carol A. Horton
Taneytown, MD

Boo!

Scare up plenty of **basic-fact practice** playing this small-group game! Cut ten or more index cards into thirds. On three cards sketch a friendly ghost and write the word "Boo!" Program the rest of the cards with unanswered math facts. Store the cards in a plastic pumpkin or trick-or-treat bag. To play, one student in the group draws a card, reads the fact aloud, and provides its answer. If the group agrees that his answer is correct, he keeps the card. If his answer is incorrect, he returns the card. Then he passes the container to the classmate on his left. Play continues in this manner. When a player draws a Boo! card, he must return all his cards to the container, including the Boo! card. The student who has the most cards at the end of game time wins. Boo!

Terri Flowers—Grs. K–2
Schochler Primary
Channelview, TX

Spooky Fact Families

Sandwiched between the covers of this haunted house is a "spook-tacular" review of **math fact families!** To make her booklet cover, a student folds a 12" x 18" sheet of black construction paper in half and cuts away the top two corners as shown. Then she writes the title "[Student name]'s Spooky Fact Families" and adds desired decorations.

For a review of ten fact families, staple five sheets of blank paper inside each child's booklet cover and have her cut away the top corners of the pages to match her cover. To ready each page for a fact family, she draws the lines shown, making an attic and four rooms. To complete each page, she writes the numbers of an assigned fact family in the attic. Then in each room she writes a different addition or subtraction problem for that family.

Mary E. Hoffman—Gr. 2
Camp Avenue Elementary
North Merrick, NY

Weighing In

Take a sweet approach to **estimating and measuring weight!** You need a balance scale, a large bowl of candy pumpkins, objects to be weighed, and student copies of a recording sheet like the one shown. Place a lightweight object, such as a pencil or clothespin, on one end of the scale. Ask each child to write on his paper the name of the object and how many candy pumpkins he thinks it weighs. Then add candies to the opposite end of the scale, counting each one out loud, until the scale is balanced. Have students record this number on their papers. Weigh a series of objects in the manner described. Encourage students to apply the knowledge they have learned from each previous weighing as they make their estimates. For a sweet conclusion, surprise students with a second bowl of candy pumpkins that are just for eating!

Amy Emmons
Enon Elementary
Franklinton, LA

Weighing With Candy Pumpkins

Object	Estimate	Actual Weight
clothespin	5 candies	

Multiplying by Two

$1 \times 2 = 2$

$2 \times 2 = 4$

$3 \times$

scratch
scratch

Two-Eyed Pumpkins

Make **multiplying by two** as easy as adding two eyes to a pumpkin! Each child traces a pumpkin template on orange construction paper and cuts out the shape. From scrap paper she cuts out a green stem and two large black eyes, and then she glues the cutouts to her pumpkin. Title a length of bulletin board paper "Multiplying by Two." Mount the pumpkins on the paper in rows, beginning with one pumpkin in the first row, two in the second row, and so on. Continue adding rows until your pumpkin supply runs out. Then, at the end of each row, write the multiplication fact the pumpkin set represents. Invite students to make additional pumpkins for the display so that you have ten pumpkin sets. Now, that's a picture-perfect understanding of multiplying by two!

Amy Emmons

Party Puzzlers

Your youngsters' **problem-solving skills** are sure to flourish on this party scene! Make student copies of page 124. Guide younger students through the activity. Challenge more capable students to complete the activity independently. If desired, give each child a letter-size envelope in which to store her picture cards for additional problem-solving fun!

adapted from an idea by Erin Harp
Manchester, NH

Barry Slate

Monster Cards Use with "Place Value Monsters" on page 120.

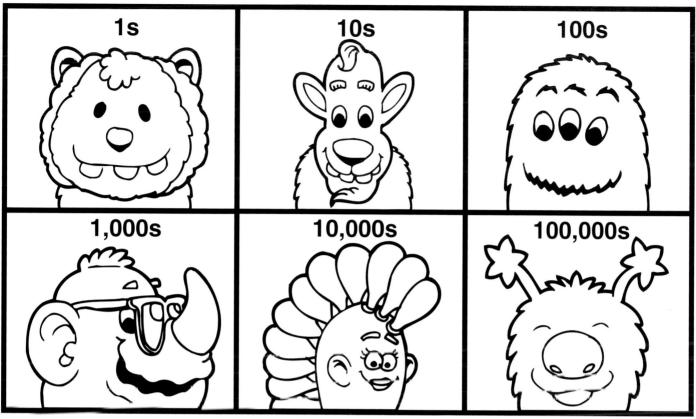

Pumpkin Planner Use with "Pumpkin Glyph" on page 121.

Pumpkin Planner

Choose the sentence that describes your leaf and then follow the direction.

Size: My leaf is smaller than my hand.   Choose a black crayon.
My leaf is larger than my hand.   Choose a yellow crayon.
My leaf is the size of my hand.   Choose a blue crayon.

Edges: My leaf has curved edges.   Color two ● eyes.
My leaf has pointy edges.   Color two ■ eyes.
My leaf has curved and pointy edges.   Color two ▲ eyes.

Stem: My leaf has a stem.   Color a ▲ nose.
My leaf does not have a stem.   Color a ● nose.

Color: My leaf is mostly red.   Color a [mouth] mouth.
My leaf is mostly yellow.   Color a [mouth] mouth.
My leaf is mostly orange.   Color a [mouth] mouth.
My leaf is mostly brown.   Color a [mouth] mouth.

To finish your pumpkin, color the stem green. Color the rest of the pumpkin orange.
Then cut out the pumpkin.

Name _____

A Costume Party

Color the pictures below and cut them out.
Use four pictures to solve each problem.
Write your answer in the blank.

1. The scarecrow came before the ghost.
   The vampire came before the scarecrow.
   The monster came after the ghost.
   Who came first?

   _____

2. The skeleton danced after the pumpkin.
   The scarecrow danced after the skeleton.
   The ghost danced before the pumpkin.
   Who danced first?

   _____

3. The pumpkin ate more than the skeleton.
   The vampire ate less than the monster.
   The pumpkin ate less than the vampire.
   Who ate the most?

   _____

4. The vampire sang louder than the monster.
   The scarecrow sang louder than the vampire.
   The ghost sang louder than the scarecrow.
   Who sang the loudest?

   _____

5. The ghost laughed more than the monster.
   The vampire laughed more than the pumpkin.
   The pumpkin laughed more than the ghost.
   Who laughed the most?

   _____

6. The monster left before the pumpkin.
   The skeleton left after the vampire.
   The vampire left after the pumpkin.
   Who left last?

   _____

Note to the teacher: Use with "Party Puzzlers" on page 122.

A MENU OF MATH

Cranberries, turkey, muffins, and more provide math activities with all the trimmings!

ideas by Stacie Stone Davis

tens | ones

A Cranberry Count

Here's a "berry" good way to practice estimation skills. Put one pound of whole cranberries into a large, clear plastic container. Ask each student to estimate the number of cranberries in the container and write his estimate on a personalized paper slip. Collect the paper slips for later use. Then, as a class, count the number of cranberries in the container. To do this you will need a large tens-and-ones chart like the one shown and several clear plastic cups. Lay the chart on the floor and have students gather around it. With your students' help, count ten cranberries into a clear plastic cup. Set the cup of cranberries on the tens column of the chart. Continue in this manner until no more groups of ten can be made; then set the remaining single cranberries on the ones column. As a group, count the tens and ones to find out how many cranberries were in the container. Then determine which student made the closest estimate.

For a fun follow-up, read aloud *Cranberry Thanksgiving* by Wende and Harry Devlin. Then, if desired, use the counted cranberries and the recipe from the book to make cranberry bread. Or make cranberry-orange relish (see the provided recipe) that can be served atop corn muffins (see "Muffin Multiplication" on page 126).

Cranberry-Orange Relish

1 pound fresh cranberries
1 orange, peeled and seeds removed
2 cups sugar
blender
spoon
mixing bowl

Combine the cranberries and the orange in the blender. When well blended, transfer the mixture to the mixing bowl. Stir in sugar to taste. Serve atop hot muffins or refrigerate until ready to serve.

Squash Circumferences

Squash, anyone? This small-group activity helps students compare the circumferences of a variety of squash. Prepare a workstation for each small group that includes a different winter squash (such as *acorn, buttercup, turban, butternut, Hubbard,* or *pumpkin*); three pieces of double-sided tape attached to a wall (or chart); three cards labeled "too short," "just right," and "too long"; scissors; and a supply of uncut string. Assign a group of students to each workstation. One at a time, each group member examines the circumference of the group's squash (at its widest point) and cuts a length of string that he thinks equals that distance. After each student has cut a length of string, have each group member wrap his cut string around the group's squash and then display his string under the appropriate card as shown. Invite each group to report on the accuracy of its estimates; then ask students if they think their estimates might have been more accurate if each group member had tested and displayed his cut string before the next group member took his turn. Discuss the advantages of making an estimate after several pieces of data have been gathered. Then, if desired, rotate the squash and repeat the activity in the manner described.

too short | just right | too long

Muffin Multiplication

Students are sure to enjoy this tasty introduction to arrays! Gather muffin tins in assorted sizes. Then, using a prepackaged mix or a favorite recipe, prepare a large batch of corn muffin batter—enlisting your students' help if desired. Divide students into small groups and give each group a muffin tin, pencils, and scrap paper. Help students see that each muffin tin is an array. Ask each group to determine a multiplication problem (or an addition problem) that its muffin tin represents. Then visit each group, place a paper liner in each muffin tin compartment, and fill the compartments with batter. After the group's muffin tin has been filled, have the group share its array-related problem(s) with the class. Continue in this manner until all the muffin tins have been filled.

While the muffins are baking, challenge each group to locate and list on their papers other classroom arrays, such as windowpanes and desk or cubby arrangements. When the muffins are done, serve them with the cranberry-orange relish prepared in "A Cranberry Count." If desired, invite another class to your corn muffin feast. While students are enjoying the muffins, read aloud the hilariously funny *'Twas the Night Before Thanksgiving* by Dav Pilkey.

Time for Turkey!

No doubt many students have heard their moms, dads, grandparents, or other relatives or friends in the kitchen on Thanksgiving Day, anxiously figuring what time the turkey needs to be put in the oven so that it's ready for dinner. Take some of the mystery out of this event with the following gobbling-good activity. Each student needs a clock manipulative with movable hands. Explain that for each pound of a large turkey, the turkey must cook about 15 minutes. Then, with your students' help, make a chart that shows the cooking times for turkeys weighing eight or more pounds.

Afterward, ask students to solve problems such as, "If a ten-pound turkey were put in the oven at noon, what time should the turkey be finished cooking?" or "If a family wants to eat at 5:00 P.M. and they have a 20-pound turkey, what time should the turkey be put in the oven?" Encourage students to use their clock manipulatives for assistance in making the chart and solving the problems.

WHERE'S THE BEEF?

Pumpkin-Pie Fractions

This activity makes reviewing fractions as easy as pie! Under your students' watchful eyes, cut a prepared pumpkin pie into eight equal slices. Put a dollop of whipped cream on one pie slice; then ask students to name how many pie slices have whipped cream. When students volunteer the answer, "One slice," explain that this answer could also be expressed as "One slice out of eight," or "one-eighth of the pie." Repeat this process until each pie slice is topped with a dollop of whipped cream. If desired repeat the process with other pies that have been divided into halves, thirds, fourths, and sixths.

For a fun follow-up activity, duplicate the patterns on page 127 onto orange construction paper. Give each child one pattern. To make her pumpkin-pie fraction project, a student colors the pie crust brown; then she cuts out the pie pattern. Next, she brushes a thin layer of glue on each section of the pie and sprinkles pumpkin pie spice onto the glue. When the project is dry, she shakes the excess spice into a provided container such as a shoebox lid. Next, she glues each white pom-pom that she has been given on a pie slice and labels a blank index card to show what fraction of her pie has been topped with "whipped cream." Verify each child's work, and collect the projects and index cards for use at a center. For a fun finale, serve each child a small portion of the sliced pumpkin pie(s) that you used to introduce this lesson.

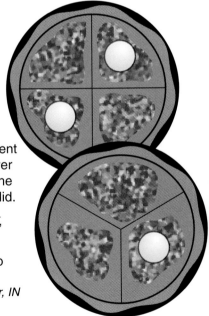

adapted from an idea by Toni Stewart, Montpelier, IN

A Shopping Extravaganza

Culminate your Thanksgiving-related math activities by having each youngster complete the reproducible activity on page 128. Students may complete the activity independently or in small groups. Have money manipulatives available to assist students.

As an extension to this activity, give each student a grocery-store circular that features Thanksgiving-type foods. (Some grocery stores may be willing to donate a class supply of circulars.) Have students use the circulars to solve teacher-created math problems that correspond to the circular. Or challenge each student to plan and determine the cost of a Thanksgiving Day dinner that uses the foods featured in his circular.

Answer Key For Page 128

1. $3.00
2. $1.55
3. $1.15
4. $2.40
5. $1.90
6. $3.50
7. $1.70
8. $1.90

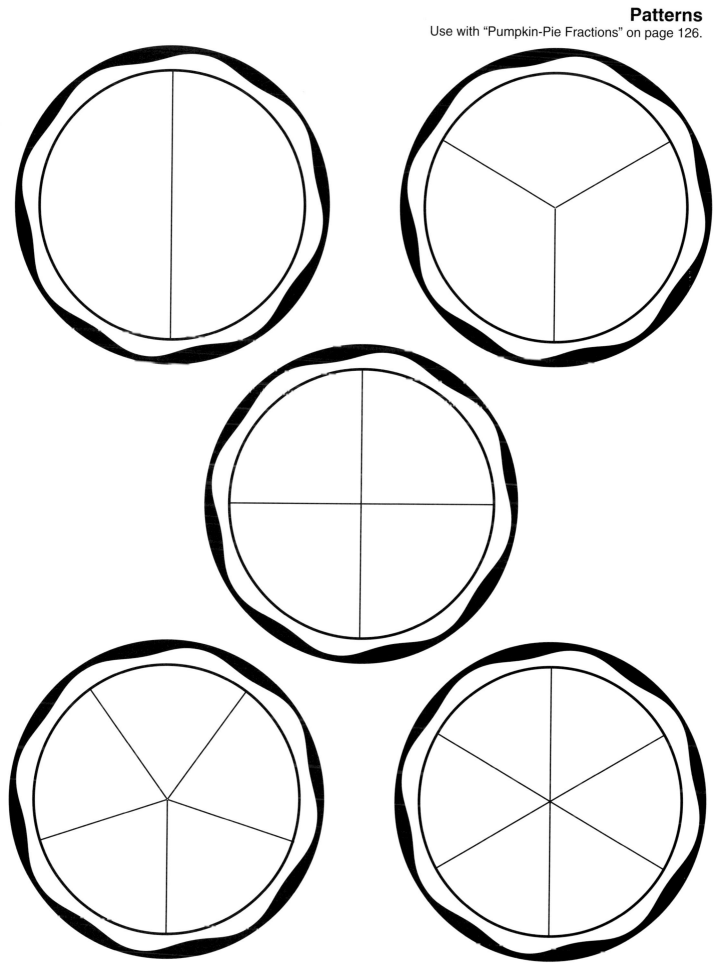

Name____

A Gobblin'-Good Sale!

Find the total of each purchase.
Show your work in the boxes.
Write your answers on the lines.

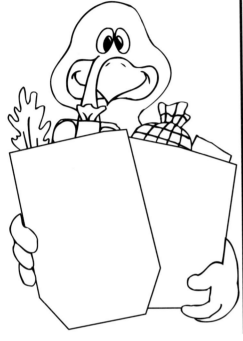

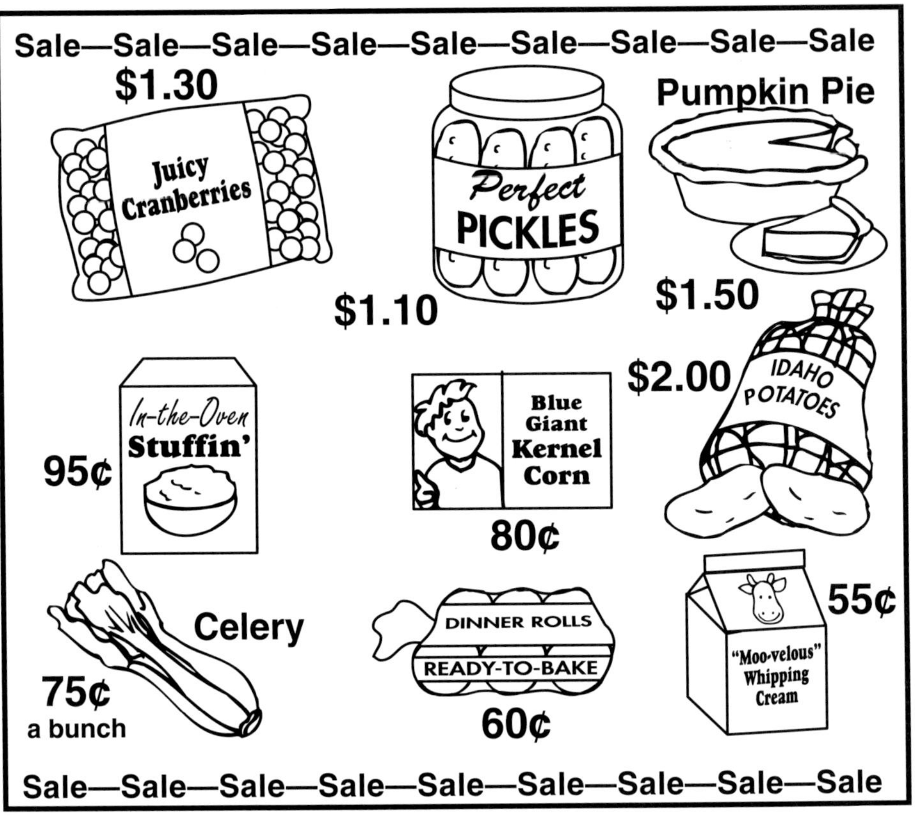

Sale—Sale—Sale—Sale—Sale—Sale—Sale—Sale—Sale
$1.30
Juicy Cranberries
Perfect PICKLES
$1.10
Pumpkin Pie
$1.50
$2.00
IDAHO POTATOES
In-the-Oven Stuffin'
95¢
Blue Giant Kernel Corn
80¢
Celery
75¢ a bunch
DINNER ROLLS READY-TO-BAKE
60¢
"Moo-velous" Whipping Cream
55¢
Sale—Sale—Sale—Sale—Sale—Sale—Sale—Sale—Sale

1. two pumpkin pies ____________
2. a bunch of celery and a box of corn ____________
3. a bag of dinner rolls and a carton of whipping cream ____________
4. a jar of pickles and a bag of cranberries ____________
5. two boxes of stuffing ____________
6. a bag of potatoes and a pumpkin pie ____________
7. a box of stuffing and a bunch of celery ____________
8. a bag of cranberries and a bag of dinner rolls ____________

1.	2.
3.	4.
5.	6.
7.	8.

 Note to the teacher: Use with "A Shopping Extravaganza" on page 126.

Hats Off to Math!

Hold on to your hat as you check out this collection of top-of-the-line math ideas! The third Friday in January is officially recognized as Hat Day, but a celebration of hats can be planned for any time of year. So don your dandiest hat and let the learning begin!

ideas by Shari Abbey, Dolores J. Behe, and Lisa Leonardi

Blake Tyler
This is a baseball cap with a red bill and white front, with a red star on it. This is the cap I wore when we won the baseball tournament.

Hat Museum

To prepare for your hat-related studies, transform part of your classroom into a hat museum. Ask each student to bring a favorite hat from home. Encourage students to consider hats that have special meaning for them. For example, a student may choose a parent's work hat, a unique decorative hat, or a hat that was purchased during a favorite vacation. Be sure to provide extra hats to ensure the participation of all students. Next, have each child label a large index card with his name, a brief description of his hat, and one or two sentences that explain why the hat is special. Display the cards and hats together for all to see.

Hats Off to Addition

This hands-on approach to basic facts is brimming with excitement! At the front of the classroom, display 11 hats from the class museum. Number the hats in order from zero to ten; then place the corresponding numbers of manipulatives under the hats. (For example, place one Unifix cube under Hat #1, and four Unifix cubes under Hat #4.) You will also need individual index cards, each labeled with a different sum from 1 to 18.

To begin, have one student randomly choose a sum card and display it for his classmates to see. Then ask students to contribute addition facts that equal the displayed sum. As you write each addition sentence on the chalkboard, have two students verify the sentence by lifting the corresponding hats and counting the manipulatives that are revealed. When all the facts for a particular sum have been identified, it's time to draw a new sum card. Student involvement makes this activity add up to lots of fun!

Hats and Hoops

Strengthen your students' sorting skills with this hands-on activity. Place two or three Hula-Hoops (or large yarn circles) on your classroom floor. Ask students to retrieve their hats from the museum and gather on the floor around the hoops. Then, as they hold their hats in their laps, challenge the students to study the hats on display and determine different ways the hats could be sorted. Under your direction, have students sort their hats into the hoops, using a variety of attributes.

Next, remove all the hoops but one and have each student place her hat outside the hoop. To play this sorting game, choose one child to be It. This child secretly chooses an attribute and begins placing the hats that have this attribute inside the hoop. The remainder of the class watches closely. When a student thinks she knows the attribute that is being used, she raises her hand. When the hats are sorted, It calls on her classmates until one student correctly identifies the sorting attribute. This student becomes the new It. The hats are removed from the hoop and the game is played again.

Keep This Under Your Hat!

Here's a math activity that will keep your youngsters guessing! Program a class set of index cards using different numbers from 10 to 100; then have each student retrieve his hat from the museum and place it on his head. Before you distribute the cards, explain that the numbers on them must be kept secret. Suggest that each student store his card under his hat once he has read his number. Then have each child write three clues about his secret number. The first clue must reveal whether the number is even or odd. The second clue must involve addition, and the third clue must involve subtraction. After the clues have been written, the detective work begins! Divide students into small groups and have each student take a turn sharing his three clues with the other detectives in his group. When a conclusion has been drawn by the detectives, the student tips his hat to reveal the correct answer!

Hats for Sale!

Students will take to this appealing variation of money-counting practice at the drop of a hat! Have each student retrieve his hat from the class museum and display it on his desk. Distribute index cards that you have labeled with different hat prices. (Tailor the prices to reflect your students' money-counting skills.) Ask students to display the price tags near their hats.

To begin the activity, divide the class into two groups—merchants and shoppers. Give each shopper a container of plastic or real coins that can be used to purchase any individual hat. Explain that the merchants will pretend to sell their hats and the shoppers will pretend to buy the hats the merchants are selling. To buy a hat, a shopper counts out coins that equal the price of the hat and gives the coins to the merchant. While the merchant is recounting the coins for accuracy, the shopper may don the hat he has purchased. If the coin amount is correct, the merchant returns the coins to the shopper and the shopper returns the hat. If there is a discrepancy in the coin amount, the merchant and shopper discuss and correct it before the coins and the hat are returned. After several purchases have been made by each shopper, have him give his container of coins to a merchant and return to his desk. Now the shoppers become merchants, the merchants become shoppers, and a second round of money-value review takes place!

More Hats for Sale!

For additional reinforcement of money skills, have students don their thinking caps and complete the reproducible on page 132. When your students have completed the activity, reward them for their efforts with a tasty top-hat treat! (See "Top-Hat Treats" on this page.)

Top-Hat Treats

Top off a hat-related math activity with these tasty student-made treats! At a center place paper napkins, plastic knives, vanilla wafers, peanut butter, a teaspoon, a ruler, and several bananas (approximately one for every three students). To prepare a top-hat treat, place a vanilla wafer on a napkin; then measure and spread one teaspoon of peanut butter atop the wafer. Next, measure and cut a two-inch portion of banana. Peel the banana and position it atop the wafer to create a tiny top hat! These unique treats are sure to measure up to your students' taste expectations!

Now, "T-hat's" a Graph!

Reading a graph could be old hat to your students by the conclusion of this activity! Ask each student to count the hats in her home. Then have the students compile their findings on a large graph like the one shown. To do this, each student writes her name on the left side of the grid and colors one square next to her name for each hat that she counted in her home. Next have students use the resulting graph to write ten number sentences that contain number comparisons like *more, less, equal, same, most, least,* and *altogether*. For more graph-reading practice, have each child read aloud two or three of her number sentences, and have the rest of the class read the graph to verify her work.

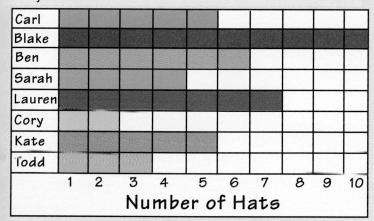

	1	2	3	4	5	6	7	8	9	10
Carl										
Blake										
Ben										
Sarah										
Lauren										
Cory										
Kate										
Todd										

Number of Hats

Place-Value Practice

Students will eagerly don their hats from the class museum to participate in this unique place-value activity! Use the digits 1 through 9 to program a class supply of index cards. Give one card to each student and have him tape the card to the front of his hat. Then select two or more students to stand before their classmates, wearing their hats. Challenge the standing students to arrange themselves so that the digits on their hats create the largest (smallest) possible number. Ask the seated students to approve each number. For more place-value practice, ask seated students to name the digits that are in specific place-value locations. When appropriate, select another group of students to gather at the front of the classroom. Continue in this manner until all students have participated.

Hat-Making Extravaganza

Who would guess that making and decorating paper hats could reinforce math skills! In advance set up a class-room store where small items for decorating hats can be purchased. Consider items like beads, buttons, feathers, glitter, pom-poms, ribbons, sequins, silk flowers, colorful paper, and wallpaper and fabric scraps. Post a price list in the store, keeping in mind the amount of money each child will be given to spend on hat-making supplies.

Refer to the illustrated steps on this page to guide students in crafting paper hats. When the hats are ready, give each student plastic or real coins of a predetermined value for purchasing hat-decorating supplies. If desired, arrange for each child to visit the classroom store one time before any purchases are made. During this visit the student lists the supplies he would like to buy and their prices. Then the student returns to his desk, totals his list to determine whether he has stayed within his spending budget, and adjusts his list as necessary. Next, arrange for small groups of students to make their purchases. Finally, have each child use his supplies to adorn his paper hat. Invite your hatmakers to wear their creations for all to see!

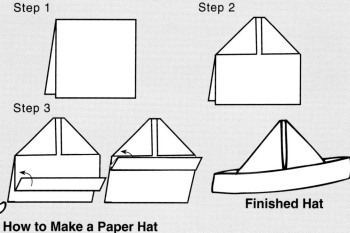

Step 1

Step 2

Step 3

Finished Hat

How to Make a Paper Hat

1. Fold a 14" x 23" sheet of newsprint in half.
2. Place the fold at the top; then fold down each top corner as shown.
3. At the lower edge, fold up the top flap twice as shown.
4. Flip the hat and repeat Step 3.

Name _____

Shopping for Hats!

Read the directions.
Add to solve.
Color.

$.35

3. _____

4. _____

$.30

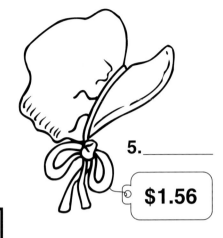

5. _____

$1.56

2. _____

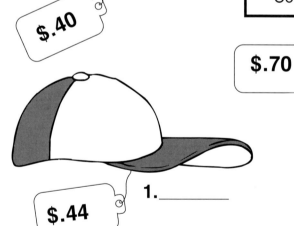

$.40

---

1. Find two tags that total $2.00.
   Color both tags green.

2. Find two tags that total $.95.
   Color both tags yellow.

3. Find two tags that total $1.05.
   Color both tags red.

4. Find two tags that total $.90.
   Color both tags orange.

5. Find two tags that total $1.25.
   Color both tags blue.

6. _____

$.90

7. _____

$.75

$.70

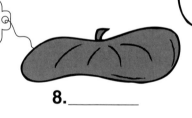

8. _____

1. _____

$.44

Match a name to each hat.
Use the list below.
Write the letters on the lines.

A. Straw hat	**F.** Top hat
B. Fireman's hat	**G.** Party hat
C. Cowboy hat	**H.** Bowler
D. Bonnet	**I.** Sailor hat
E. Beret	**J.** Baseball cap

$.50

10. _____

$.25

9. _____

Exploring Math in the Great Outdoors

Give your math review a creative twist by heading outdoors! A healthy dose of fresh air and sunshine is the perfect way to rejuvenate and reinforce a variety of math skills!

ideas contributed by Monica Cavender

Warming Up to Math

Set the stage for outdoor math adventures by gathering students around an imaginary campfire. Explain that math is all around, even in the great outdoors! Invite youngsters to share examples of math in their everyday environments. Then, if possible, read aloud *Math Curse* by Jon Scieszka. This experience around the campfire is sure to spark an interest in outdoor math!

Gearing Up

Take a few minutes to gear up your math scouts for outdoor adventure! Explain that in addition to her math expertise, each scout can use a pair of math-spotting binoculars and a scouting journal. Then refer to the following directions to lead students in making their supplies. (*To incorporate math skills, have students measure and cut these items.)

Math-Spotting Binoculars

Supplies to make one pair:
two 9-oz. Dixie cold cups
clear tape
18" length of yarn*
pencil
access to a hole puncher

Directions:
1. Use the point of the pencil to pierce the bottom of each cup; then carefully tear away the bottom of each cup.
2. Hold the cups side by side. Tape the top rims together.
3. Tape the bottom rims of the cups together; then hole-punch the outside edges of each bottom rim as shown.
4. Securely tie one end of the yarn length in each punched hole.
5. Wear (and use) your math-spotting binoculars during outdoor math adventures!

Scouting Journal

Supplies to make one:
1 copy of the cover pattern from page 137
four 6" x 18" sheets of drawing paper*
14" length of raffia (or twine)*
scissors
access to a hole puncher
crayons or markers
glue

Directions:
1. Stack and align the drawing paper; then fold the stack in half.
2. Punch two holes at the top of the stack, near the fold. (Provide assistance as needed.)
3. Thread the raffia through the holes, tie, and fashion a bow from the ends.
4. Color and personalize the cover pattern. Cut it out and glue it to the front of the journal.
5. Complete outdoor math activities in your journal as directed by your teacher.

Estimating the Distance

An outdoor hike is just what your scouts need to sharpen their estimation skills! Before heading outdoors, ask each child to sketch a chart in his journal like the one shown. Then gather students at a designated class campsite near the edge of the playground and divide them into five groups. Select five playground objects that are comparable distances from the class campsite and assign one to each group. Each scout estimates how many steps it will take him to walk from the class campsite to his group's object and writes his estimate on his chart. Next, he counts his steps as he hikes to the object. He records this number on his chart and returns to the class campsite.

Instruct students to complete their charts in a like manner, by first estimating the number of movements needed to reach the object, counting the movements, and then recording the actual count. Encourage them to evaluate the data they've recorded before they make a new estimate, as this can help them sharpen their estimation skills. In conclusion, have the students in each group compare their findings, discuss which methods of movement were easiest (most difficult) to estimate, and propose reasons why actual counts may differ among group members.

To Oak Tree	Estimate	Actual Number
steps		
lunges		
hops		
skips		

Shape Spotters

Watch your scouts' geometry skills take shape during this outdoor expedition! In advance, review the names and attributes of the basic shapes introduced during the school year. Then lead the class around the school grounds. Ask each scout to search for objects that represent the shapes reviewed and record his findings in his journal. After you return to the classroom, list on the chalkboard the different sightings of each shape. Accept all reasonable answers. Next, have each scout choose a different item from the chalkboard to illustrate on provided paper. While students work, label a sheet of poster board for each shape being reviewed. Then have each child glue his illustration to the appropriate poster. Display the shapely projects around the classroom for all to see. Invite students to add illustrations to the posters as they spot additional shapes in the great outdoors!

Circles

Pattern Trails

The great outdoors is the perfect place to find manipulatives for patterning practice. Have each child collect small loose items—such as fallen leaves and twigs, pieces of grass, and stones—in a paper lunch bag. Then have each child use the items she collects to create one or more patterns. Ask each child to illustrate her favorite pattern in her journal. For an added challenge, have students keep a tally of how many different patterns they can make using the items they've collected.

Searching for Sums

Reinforce addition skills with an outdoor sum search! To prepare, list on the chalkboard ten different basic fact sums. Ask each scout to copy the sums near the top of a journal page. Then take the scouts outdoors to search for items that add up to each sum. When a student finds a sum, he writes and solves a number sentence in his journal (see illustration). Then he marks out the sum on his original list. Challenge students to find each listed sum within an allotted amount of time. Now, that's "sum" fun!

Kellie Henry—Gr. 3
St. Joseph Grade School
St. Joseph, IL

Outdoor Ordinals

Polish ordinal skills with this outdoor challenge! Label half of a class set of cards with ordinal numbers through "tenth." Label the remaining cards to match. Shuffle each resulting deck. Have an adult helper arrange a line of ten plastic cones in a grassy outdoor area, leaving ample space between them. Have the adult helper take half of the students, a deck of cards, and scorekeeping materials to one end of the cones. Take the remaining students and similar supplies to the opposite end.

To play, each adult simultaneously announces the first ordinal number in her deck. The first player in line jogs to the corresponding cone and touches it. Then he jogs back to the team and asks, "Did I touch the correct cone?" If the team responds "yes," he earns two points and goes to the end of the line. If the team responds, "Choose a friend," he selects a teammate and the pair repeats his turn, making sure the correct cone is touched. When the twosome returns, one point is added to the team score. The friend returns to her place in line and the original player goes to the end of the line. The adult then announces the next ordinal number in the deck. Play continues in a like manner until all cards have been played. The team with more points wins. When both teams score equal points, both teams win!

adapted from an idea by Sammie Hardy—Grs. 1–5
Goodrich Elementary
Goodrich, TX

Lively Skip-Counting

This mathematical version of hopscotch hones skip-counting skills! On a paved outdoor surface, use chalk to draw a gameboard like the one shown. Divide students into two groups and have one group line up at each end of the gameboard. Call out a desired multiple and point to Line 1. The first person in Line 1 hops through the gameboard as her classmates skip-count by the number called. When she reaches the end of the gameboard, she proceeds to the end of Line 2 as the first person in Line 2 hops back through the pattern to his classmates' counting. When he reaches the end of the gameboard, the round is over. He walks to the end of Line 1, a different multiple is announced, and another round of hopping and counting begins.

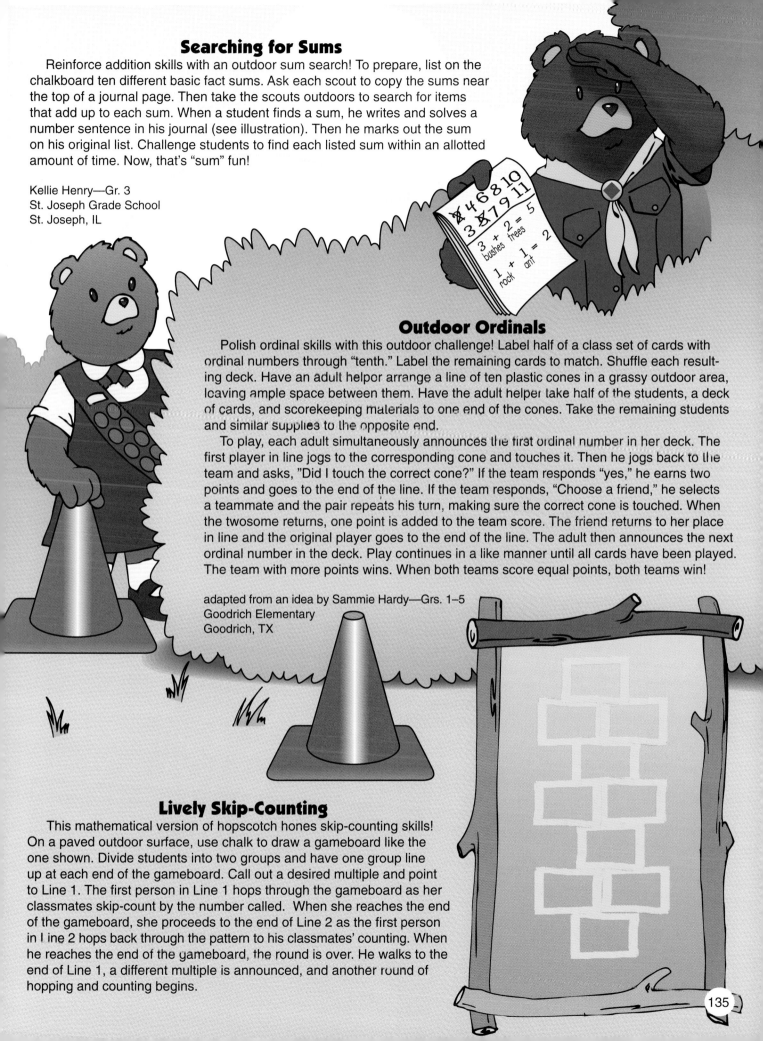

Fractional Finds

A review of fractions is just a step away! If desired, read aloud *Fraction Action* by Loreen Leedy to review fractional parts of sets. Then head outdoors and arrange your scouts in a horizontal line. Ask each of four scouts to take a giant step forward and then turn to face the class. Lead the remainder of the class in counting the number of classmates in this set. Next, ask individual students to use fractions to describe how many boys (girls) are in the set, how many students in the set are wearing sneakers, and so on. Then have the set of four return to the class line. Repeat the activity a number of times, choosing different students and varying the size of the sets. Continue until each scout has been a part of a set one or more times. When the class is back in the classroom, ask each scout to illustrate and label a favorite fraction from this outdoor experience.

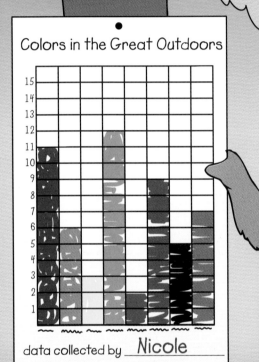

Colorful Data

Colorful bar graphs result from this outdoor math adventure! To begin, have each child draw lines to divide two journal pages into four sections each. Then have her label the eight resulting sections with the following color words: red, orange, yellow, green, blue, purple, black, and brown. Next, lead your scouts to an outdoor area where they can sit comfortably. Instruct them to quietly observe their surroundings for colors that appear in nature. Then, in their journals, have them list the objects they see by color. Return to the classroom at a predetermined time and give each child a bar graph like the one shown. Ask each child to organize the data she collected on the graph. Set aside time for students to compare the results of their work; then, as a class, discuss why the results of this graphing experience differ.

Bloomin' Calculations

Computation skills are sure to blossom with this thought-provoking activity! If possible, take your scouts outdoors to observe real flowers. Then have each child illustrate in his journal a flower with several individual petals. Next, ask him to count the petals on the flower he drew, write this number on the page, and circle it. Finally, challenge each scout to write multiple math equations in his journal that equal the circled number. Encourage students to be creative! After a predetermined amount of time, pair students and have each child check his partner's work. Now, that's a creative approach to computation practice!

Exploring Math in the
Great Outdoors

Data Collected by _____

Math Scout

Math Scout
Merit Badge

Math Scout
Merit Badge

Note to the teacher: Use the cover pattern with "Gearing Up: Scouting Journal" on page 133. Copy one merit badge on construction paper for each child. Upon completion of a desired number of outdoor math activities, award each math scout a merit badge to color and cut out.

Number World
A Theme Park for Mathematicians

For a kid-pleasing, math review, visit Number World! There's no other theme park like it!

ideas contributed by Linda Masternak Justice

Rides at Number World

Monster Wave	▮▮
Rockin' Roller Coaster	▮▮▮▮▮
The Screaming Cyclone	▮▮▮▮▮▮
Twin Twirling Cups	▮
Thunder Wheel	▮▮▮
Speedy Steeds	▮▮

Fact-o Wheel

Reviewing basic facts is as easy as taking a spin on the fact-o wheel. And word has it that one ride is never enough! For each ride on the fact-o wheel, make a copy of page 140 and program the hub of the wheel with a desired operation and number. Copy the programmed page for students. (If desired, make an extra copy and use it to make an answer key.) To keep your students' mathematical wheels turning, provide a different basic fact review each day!

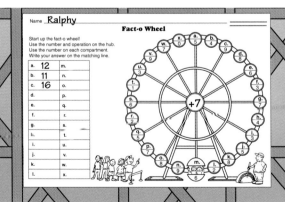

Tickets to Ride

Most every theme park has rides, and Number World is no exception! Find out which rides your students prefer with this pictograph activity. List the names of several fictional rides on a length of bulletin board paper and give each child two tickets. Invite students to suggest, based on its name, what each ride might be like. Next, ask each child to select the two rides he would most like to try. Then, in turn, have each youngster tape his tickets to the bulletin board paper to show the two rides he has selected. Have students study the completed pictograph to determine the most and least popular rides. Then have them use the information on the graph to create and solve a variety of word problems.

Flashy Bumper Cars

The bumper cars at Number World don't crash and bang. Instead they provide a fraction skills tune-up! Give each child a copy of page 141 and let the fun begin!

Take a Seat!

If 11 best friends visit a carnival (or Number World), how can they ride together on the same rides? Stuart J. Murphy has the answers in his book *Divide and Ride*. Give each child 11 squares of paper—one for each best friend. Then read the book aloud, pausing after each seating arrangement is described. Allow time for students to use their manipulatives to solve the seating predicament, and then reveal the solution that is provided. Now, that's a review of division that just might come in handy this summer!

Ridin' the Rails

There's a reason roller coasters are called scream machines! But never fear—this activity results in number order, not shrieks! Cut a supply of 1½" x 2" cards from different colors of construction paper. Using numbers appropriate for your students, label each card with a different number. Randomly distribute the cards—five per child. Pair students. Instruct each child to organize his cards numerically and then have his partner check his work. Next, instruct the twosome to combine its cards and sequence them. At this point, group each pair with another pair, forming groups of four. Ask the members of each small group to combine and then sequence their cards. Verify each group's work. Then give each group a length of bulletin board paper, glue, and crayons or markers. Have each group of students glue its sequenced cards end to end on the paper, as if they are the cars of a roller coaster. To complete the project, the members draw a track for the cars and name the roller coaster they've made!

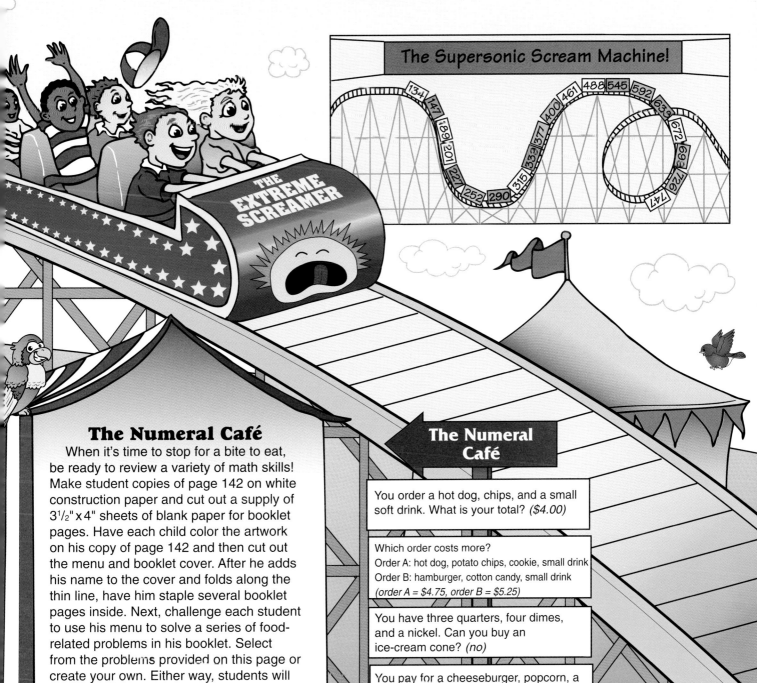

The Numeral Café

When it's time to stop for a bite to eat, be ready to review a variety of math skills! Make student copies of page 142 on white construction paper and cut out a supply of 3½" x 4" sheets of blank paper for booklet pages. Have each child color the artwork on his copy of page 142 and then cut out the menu and booklet cover. After he adds his name to the cover and folds along the thin line, have him staple several booklet pages inside. Next, challenge each student to use his menu to solve a series of food-related problems in his booklet. Select from the problems provided on this page or create your own. Either way, students will be putting their math skills to good use.

The Numeral Café

You order a hot dog, chips, and a small soft drink. What is your total? *($4.00)*

Which order costs more?
Order A: hot dog, potato chips, cookie, small drink
Order B: hamburger, cotton candy, small drink
(order A = $4.75, order B = $5.25)

You have three quarters, four dimes, and a nickel. Can you buy an ice-cream cone? *(no)*

You pay for a cheeseburger, popcorn, a candy bar, and a large drink with a ten dollar bill. What is your change? *($3.50)*

Name _____

Fact-o Wheel

Start up the fact-o wheel!
Use the number and operation on the hub.
Use the number on each compartment.
Write your answer on the matching line.

Wheel compartments:
- e. 6
- f. 3
- g. 7
- h. 4
- d. 8
- i. 3
- c. 9
- j. 5
- b. 4
- k. 8
- a. 5
- l. 2
- x. 0
- m. 6
- w. 7
- n. 9
- v. 9
- o. 8
- u. 3
- p. 7
- t. 1
- q. 5
- s. 6
- r. 2

a.		m.	
b.		n.	
c.		o.	
d.		p.	
e.		q.	
f.		r.	
g.		s.	
h.		t.	
i.		u.	
j.		v.	
k.		w.	
l.		x.	

Note to the teacher: Use with "Fact-o Wheel" on page 138.

Name _____

Cool Bumper Cars

Follow the directions.
Decorate each bumper car.

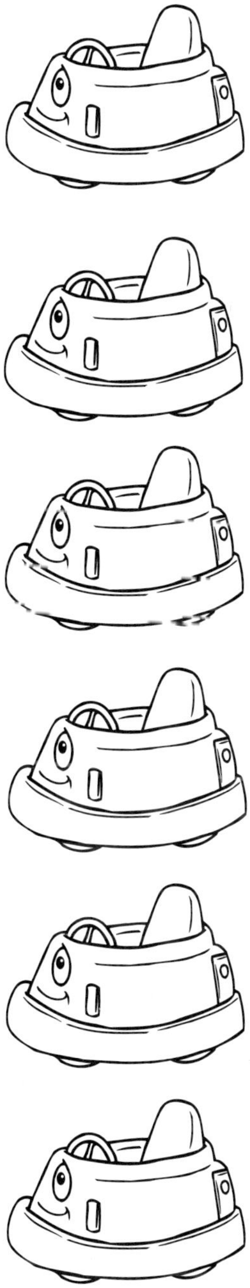

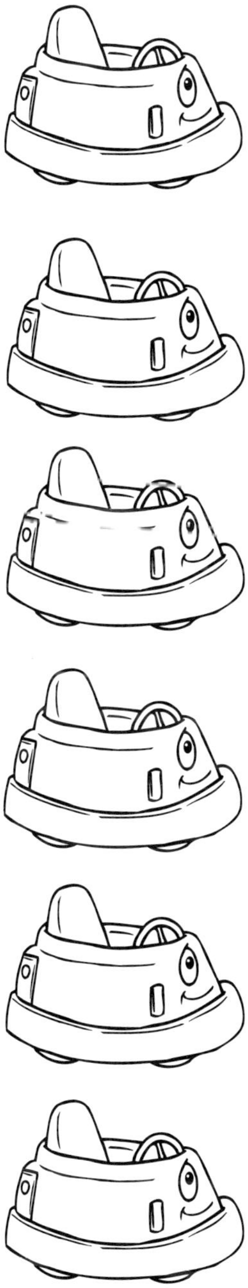

1. There are 12 blank cars.
   ½ of 12 is _____.
   Draw a yellow star on one-half of the cars.

2. Now there are 6 blank cars.
   ⅓ of 6 is _____.
   Draw a red stripe on one-third of the blank cars.

3. Now there are 4 blank cars.
   ¼ of 4 is _____.
   Draw a blue triangle on one-quarter of the blank cars.

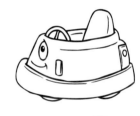

4. Now there are 3 blank cars.
   ⅔ of 3 is _____.
   Draw a purple square on two-thirds of the blank cars.

5. Now there is 1 blank car.
   Draw an orange circle on it.

6. Think about all 12 cars. Write a fraction in each blank.

   a. _____ of the cars have a purple square.
   b. _____ of the cars have a yellow star.
   c. _____ of the cars have a blue triangle.
   d. _____ of the cars have an orange circle.
   e. _____ of the cars have a red stripe.

Bonus Box: Color the bumpers on the cars. Use three different colors. Color each bumper one color. Then, on the back of this page, write three math sentences that tell about the bumper cars' bumpers!

Note to the teacher: Use with "Flashy Bumper Cars" on page 138.

Patterns

Use with "The Numeral Café" on page 139.

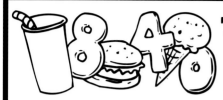

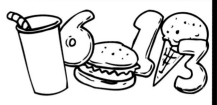

The Numeral Café Menu

Hot Dog	$1.75
Hamburger	$2.25
Cheeseburger	$2.50
Pizza Slice	$1.75
French Fries	$1.25
Potato Chips	$ .75
Peanuts	$ .50
Popcorn	$1.00
Ice-Cream Cone	$2.00
extra scoop	$ .50
Cotton Candy	$1.50
Snow Cone	$1.00
Cookie	$ .75
Candy Bar	$1.00
Soft Drink small	$1.50
large	$2.00

The Numeral Café

Solutions by ____________________

©The Education Center, Inc. • *The Best of* The Mailbox® *Math* • *Book 2* • TEC1491

©The Education Center, Inc. • *The Best of* The Mailbox® *Math* • *Book 2* • TEC1491

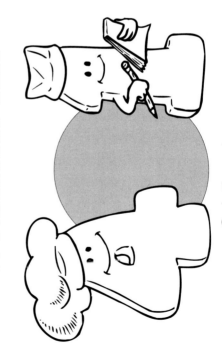

Mind or Machine

Stage a showdown between mind and machine with this calculator contest. Select one cowhand to operate a calculator, the *machine,* and one cowhand to represent the *mind.* To start the round, state a math fact for the two contestants to solve. The child with the calculator must use it even if he knows the correct answer. The first contestant to announce the correct answer earns a point for either the machine or the mind. Record the point earned on the chalkboard; then continue play as described until every youngster has participated as both the mind and the machine. (Establish a rotation system for easy management.) Your buckaroos may be surprised by the outcome of this race—and who knows? They might even agree that memorizing math facts isn't such a bad idea!

Shari Abbey—Gr. 3, Abilene Elementary School, Valley Center, KS

Add 'Em Up!

Recycle leftover book-order forms with this pardner activity. Pair cowpokes and give each child an unused book-order form to fill out. If desired, designate how many books each cowpoke may order. Then have each youngster total his order using a calculator and record the sum on his order form. Next, have each child exchange book orders with his pardner and check the total of his pardner's order for accuracy. The activity is over when the pardners agree that the sum of each of their orders is correct. To extend the fun, have each buckaroo increase his order by a designated number of books and repeat the activity. Or for an added challenge, have the pardners work together to determine a book order that equals a predetermined sum or a sum that is less than (or more than) an approved sum. Yee-haw!

Peg Good—Gr. 2, East Pike Elementary School, Indiana, PA

"Cow-culating" Averages

How does a cow know the average temperature of the past five days? She "cow-culates" it! And your buckaroos can too! At a designated time, for five consecutive days, enlist your youngsters' help in reading the outside temperature and recording it on a class chart. After the fifth temperature has been recorded, have each student use a calculator to find the sum of the temperatures. Then instruct the students to divide their sums by five to find the average daily temperature. Next, ask students how they might find the average temperature over ten days, three weeks, or a month. Then, as a class, make plans to continue reading and recording the temperature for a chosen number of days, enlisting the help of students who live nearby to read the temperature on the weekends. Don't be surprised if your buckaroos get so carried away that they're calculating average temperatures on a daily basis!

Mary Hemp—Gr. 3, Renick R–V School, Renick, MO

Rip-Roaring Riddles

Keep your young cowpokes on their toes with David A. Adler's book *Calculator Riddles.* The answer to each riddle is given as a number sentence. To find the real riddle answer, a student uses a calculator to solve the number sentence, then turns the calculator upside down and reads his answer in the display window. A riddle a day is a great way to reinforce any cowpoke's calculator skills—even your own!

Name _____

Cowpoke "Cow-culations"

Use the code.
Write a number in each shape.
Then use a calculator to solve each problem.

Code

74	45	33
16	27	91
52	10	68

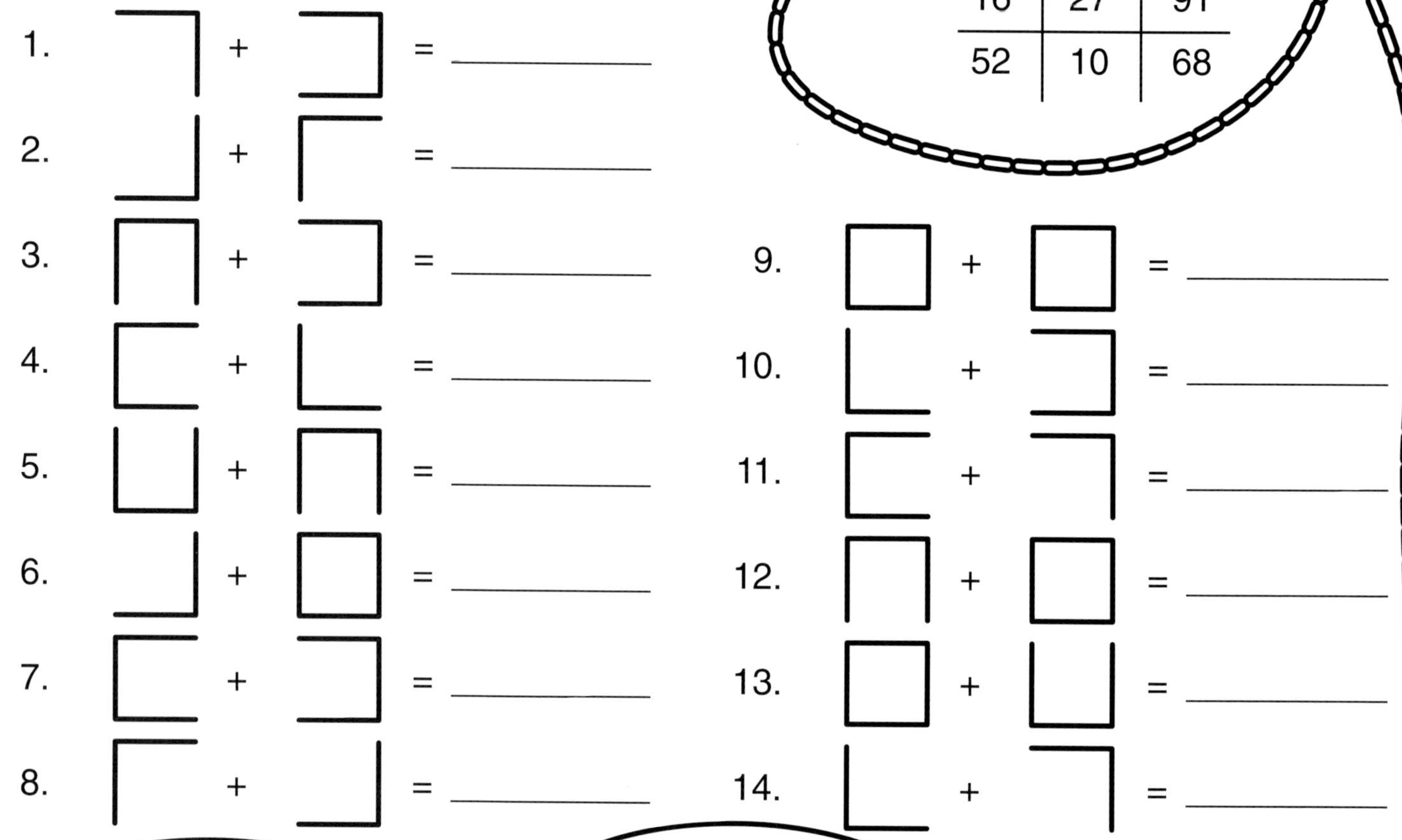

1. ⌐ + ⌐ = _____

2. ⌐ + ⌐ = _____

3. □ + □ = _____

4. ⌐ + ⌐ = _____

5. □ + ⌐ = _____

6. ⌐ + □ = _____

7. □ + ⌐ = _____

8. ⌐ + ⌐ = _____

9. □ + □ = _____

10. ⌐ + ⌐ = _____

11. ⌐ + ⌐ = _____

12. □ + □ = _____

13. □ + ⌐ = _____

14. ⌐ + ⌐ = _____

Here is an example.
$\boxed{45} + \boxed{27} = 72$

Be sure to clear your calculator after each problem!

Howdy, pardner!
On another sheet of paper, draw a new code. Put numbers in the code too! Then use the code to write a page of problems. Ask a pardner to use a calculator to solve them. When your pardner is finished, use a calculator to check your pardner's work. Yee-haw!

Note to the teacher: To extend the use of this calculator page, make a copy of the page and white-out the numbers in the code. Then reprogram the page (or a copy of it) with another set of code numbers.

It's in the Cards!

A Honey of a Math Review

What's all the buzz about? Math! You'll have a happy hive when you introduce these math review games.

ideas contributed by Sr. Helen Teresa and Marla Hawthorne

Busy Bee Cards

Each of the following games requires playing cards. The busy bee cards on page 149 are provided for your convenience. Simply duplicate the cards on construction paper or tagboard, laminate them for durability, and then cut them out. Make one set for each child or make several sets and store them at a center. Regular playing cards may also be used to play these games. Remind students to use pencil and paper for scorekeeping.

Spill a Sum
(Column addition)

Players: Two to four
Materials: Scrap paper and pencil for each player, busy bee cards 1 to 10, paper lunch bag
Directions: In turn, each player puts the cards in the bag; then he closes the bag and gently shakes it. Next, he spills the cards onto the playing surface and adds the values of the cards that land faceup. The player with the highest sum wins the round and scores one game point. If there's a tie, each player scores a point. Continue play in this manner. The first player to score five game points wins.

What's the Difference?
(Subtraction facts to 10)

Players: Two to four
Materials: Scrap paper and pencil for each player, busy bee cards 1 to 10
Directions: Shuffle the cards and stack them facedown in the center of the playing area. Each player draws one card from the stack; then each player draws a second card from the stack. In turn, each player shows her two cards, states the values on the cards as a subtraction fact, and answers the fact. The player with the lowest difference wins the round and scores one game point. If there's a tie, each player scores a point. Continue play in this manner. Reshuffle and stack discarded cards as needed. The first player to score five game points wins.

Build a Number
(Place value)

Players: Two to four
Materials: Scrap paper and pencil for each player, busy bee cards 1 to queen
Directions: Shuffle the cards and stack them facedown in the center of the playing area. Face cards are wild. Each player draws one card from the stack; then each player draws a second card from the stack. A player uses her two cards to create the largest number possible. The player with the largest number wins the round and scores one game point. If there's a tie, each player scores a point. Continue play in this manner. Reshuffle and stack discarded cards as needed. The first player to score five game points wins.

Right on the Money
(Odd and even numbers, adding money)

Players: Two to four
Materials: Scrap paper and pencil for each player, busy bee cards 1 to queen
Directions: Shuffle the cards. Even cards = 5¢, odd cards = 10¢, and face cards = 25¢. The dealer deals three cards to each player. Each player totals the value of her cards. The player with the largest value wins the round and scores one game point. If there's a tie, each player scores a game point. Continue play in this manner. Reshuffle and redeal discarded cards as needed. The first player to score five game points wins.

Make Ten
(Addition)

Players: Two
Materials: One set of busy bee cards (1 to queen) for each player
Directions: The dealer shuffles the combined cards and then he deals each player five cards. He stacks the rest of the cards facedown in a chance pile. The object of the game is to make sums of ten from pairs of cards. Face cards equal zero or ten. In turn, each player checks his hand for a card pair that equals ten. If he has one or more pairs, he lays each pair faceup on the playing surface in front of him and his turn is over. If a player does not have a pair that equals ten, he draws the top card from the chance pile. Play continues in this manner with each player laying a pair down or drawing one card during his turn. When all the cards in the chance pile are drawn, a player draws from his opponent's hand. When no more pairs can be made, the player with the most pairs of ten wins the game.

Sum It Up
(Addition)

Players: Two
Materials: One set of busy bee cards (1 to queen) per player
Directions: The dealer shuffles all 24 cards and lays them facedown between himself and his opponent. Each player selects two cards and announces their sum. Face cards equal zero. The player who has the larger sum puts all four cards in his hive (or win pile). If the sums are equal, each player puts his own cards in his hive. Play continues in this manner until all cards have been selected. The player with the most cards in his hive wins.

Subtract, Then Add
(Addition and subtraction)

Players: Two
Materials: Paper, pencil, and one set of busy bee cards (1 to queen) for each player
Directions: The dealer shuffles all 24 cards and deals them out. Each player stacks his 12 cards facedown in front of him. Each player turns over the top card in his stack. Face cards equal zero. The player with the higher card scores the difference between the two cards and records his score. (For example, if a five and three are showing, the player with the five scores two points.) These cards are placed in a discard pile. Play continues in the manner described until all cards have been played. Then each player tallies his score. The player with the higher score wins.

Count Down
(Subtraction)

Players: Two
Materials: Paper, pencil, and one set of busy bee cards (1 to queen) for each player
Directions: Combine the cards, shuffle them, and stack them facedown. Each player writes the number 25 at the top of her paper. In turn, each player draws a card from the stack. She subtracts the value of the card from 25 to determine her score. Face cards equal zero. Play continues in this manner. Reshuffle and stack discarded cards as needed. The first player to lose all her points wins.

Make a Number Sentence
(Problem solving)

Players: Two to four
Materials: Scrap paper, pencil, and one set of busy bee cards (1 to queen) per player
Directions: The dealer collects and shuffles cards and then deals each player five cards. Face cards are wild. Each player tries to make a math equation using the cards he has been dealt. Addition, subtraction, or multiplication can be used. (For example, a player with the cards 7, 3, and 4 could make the equation 7 – 3 = 4. A player with two 7s and a wild card [or a 4 and a 9] could make the equation 7 x 7 = 49.) In turn, each player shows his equation or he passes. A correct equation earns one point. All cards are then passed to a new dealer, who reshuffles and redeals them. The first player to score five points wins the game.

High or Low
(Multiplication facts)

Players: Two to four
Materials: Scrap paper and pencil for each player, busy bee cards 1 to 10
Directions: The dealer shuffles the cards, announces "high game" or "low game," and deals each player one card. Then he stacks the remaining cards in the center of the playing area and turns the top card on the stack faceup. This is the game card. Each player multiplies the number on his card with the number on the game card. If the dealer has called "high game," the player with the largest product wins the round and scores a point. (For "low game," the player with the lowest product wins the round.) If there's a tie, each player scores a game point. Continue play in this manner. Reshuffle and stack discarded cards as needed. The first player to score five game points wins.

Buzzing Into Summer
Keep your busy bees buzzing with math enthusiasm all summer long! To do this, send each child home for the summer with two sets of busy bee cards (the maximum number of cards required to play any two-person game), a copy of the games in this collection, and a letter to the parent in which you suggest that each child teach his family members and friends how to play the math games included. Now, that's a honey of an idea that's sure to please the whole hive!

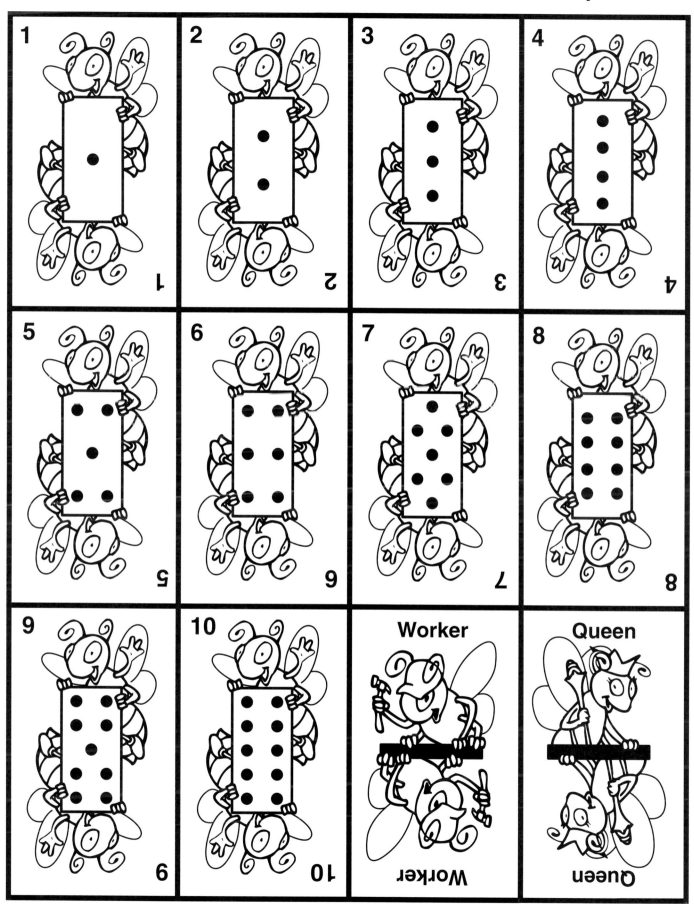

Note to the teacher: Use with "It's in the Cards!" on pages 145–148.

Learning Centers

Pumpkin Place Value

Harvest a crop of **place-value** practice with these pumpkin puzzles. Program each of several pumpkin cutouts with a numeral and a corresponding set of tens and ones as shown. Laminate the cutouts; then use a different jigsaw-style cut to separate the programming on each pumpkin cutout. Store the cutouts in a resealable plastic bag. A student removes the cutouts from the bag and pieces together the pumpkins. Now, that's a patch of prizewinning pumpkins!

Michele Lasky Anszelowicz—Gr. 1
Mandalay Elementary School
Wantagh, NY

Place-Value Practice

This daily math center is the place to reinforce **beginning place-value** skills! For each child staple a supply of blank 9" x 12" paper between two 9" x 12" construction paper covers. Have each child personalize his journal and store it in his desk or another desired location. At the center place several rubber stamps and colorful stamp pads. Each day post a different two-digit number at the center. A student takes his journal to the center and copies the posted number at the top of a blank page. Then he uses a rubber stamp and a stamp pad to program the page with a corresponding set of tens and ones as shown. You can count on this center making a lasting impression on your students!

Michele Lasky Anszelowicz—Gr. 1
Mandalay Elementary School, Wantagh, NY

Number Spin-Off

Here's a partner game that takes students' **counting** skills for a spin! Cut apart a duplicated hundreds chart and mount it on poster board as shown. Also visually divide a tagboard circle into five sections and number them 1 to 5. Laminate the resulting gameboard and spinner wheel. Snap a loose spinner in the center of the spinner wheel; then place the assembled spinner, the gameboard, and two game markers at a center. To play, the partners place their game markers on "1." Then, in turn, each child spins the spinner, moves (in numerical order) the corresponding number of spaces, and reads aloud the number he lands on. The first partner to reach 100 wins!

Kim Wachtel—Gr. 1, Sacandaga Elementary School, Scotia, NY

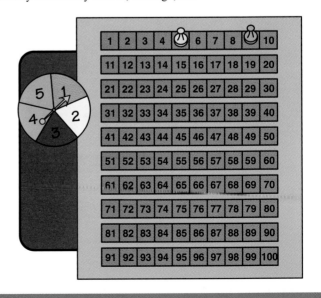

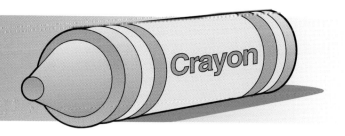

Caterpillar Count

Watch **skip-counting** skills grow right along with these cute caterpillars! To make a caterpillar for skip-counting, cut away the lid of an egg carton and then cut apart the individual egg cups. Turn each cup over. Decorate one to resemble a caterpillar head, and program the remaining cups for skip-counting. (Set aside or add extra egg cups as needed.) For self-checking, number the inside of the programmed cups in order (1, 2, 3, ...). Store the cups for each caterpillar in a labeled container or color-code each caterpillar. Working from left to right, a student arranges each set of cups in sequential order, starting with the caterpillar's head. To check his work, he inverts the caterpillar.

Nancy Y. Karpyk—Gr. 2, Broadview Elementary, Weirton, WV

Boning Up

Dish up plenty of practice with **odd and even numbers!** Label construction paper dog bone patterns with odd and even numbers; then laminate the patterns and cut them out. To program the cutouts for self-checking, use a permanent marker to draw an *X* on the back of each even-numbered bone and an *O* on the back of each odd-numbered bone. Store the cutouts in a clean and empty dog bone box. Place the box at a center along with two dog dishes labeled "Odd" and "Even." A student sorts the bones into the dishes and then flips the cutouts to check her work.

Amy Ekmark—Gr. 1
Eastside Elementary School
Lancaster, CA

Odd or Even?

Reinforce the concepts of **odd and even** at this easy-to-create center. Store blank paper, pencils, a pair of dice, and a supply of colorful peel-and-stick dots at a center. A student visually divides a sheet of blank paper into two columns and labels one column "Odd" and the other column "Even." Next, the youngster rolls the dice and determines whether the number he rolled is odd or even. He then creates and labels a matching dot set in the appropriate column of his paper. He continues in this manner until he has three or more different dot sets in each column.

Kim Wong—Gr. 2
Olney Elementary School
Olney, MD

Fact-Family Fun

Now you can deliver **fact-family practice** at a moment's notice! Place a container of dominoes, drawing paper, and pencils at a center. A student folds a sheet of paper in half twice, unfolds the paper, and letters the four resulting boxes from A to D. To complete each box, he selects and illustrates a domino. He writes the two numbers from the domino as an addition fact and supplies the answer. Then he writes the three remaining number sentences in this fact family. Now, that adds up to a whole lot of family fun!

Trudy White—Gr. 2
Mayflower Elementary
Mayflower, AR

A.
$5 + 3 = 8$
$3 + 5 = 8$
$8 - 5 = 3$
$8 - 3 = 5$

B.
$1 + 4 = 5$
$4 + 1 = 5$
$5 - 1 = 4$
$5 - 4 = 1$

C.
$6 + 2 = 8$
$2 + 6 = 8$
$8 - 2 = 6$
$8 - 6 = 2$

D.
$2 + 3 = 5$
$3 + 2 = 5$
$5 - 2 = 3$
$5 - 3 = 2$

Fishing for Fact Families

Reel in **fact families** at this math center! Label each of four fish cutouts with the numbers of a different fact family. Laminate the cutouts and then use a permanent marker to program the back of each one for self-checking. Place the fish, a supply of blank paper, pencils, crayons, and scissors at a center. A student draws four fish on her paper and copies a different fact family on each one. Then, in individual bubbles above each fish, she writes the math sentences for that family. After she checks her work, she colors the underwater scene and, if desired, trims the top of her paper to resemble waves.

Debbie Hicks—Gr. 2
White Plains Elementary
Mount Airy, NC

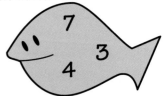

Soup-Bowl Facts

Warm students up to **math-fact** practice with bowls and beans! Use a permanent marker to program several disposable soup bowls with addition and subtraction facts; then program the bottom of each bowl with its corresponding answer. Partially fill a pot with dried beans. Place the pot, the programmed soup bowls, and a spoon at a center. A student selects a bowl, reads the fact, and uses the bean manipulatives to solve the fact in the bowl. Then she carefully lifts the bowl to check her work. If her answer is correct, she pours the beans back into the pot. If her answer is incorrect, she adjusts her bean calculation before she returns the beans. The student continues in this manner until each math fact has been completed. Soup's on!

Kristin McLaughlin—Gr. 1, Daniel Boone Area School District
Boyertown, PA

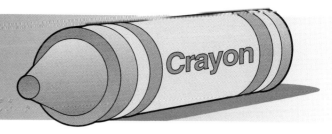

Mouthwatering Math

Sweeten your students' **basic fact recall** at this pick-of-the-patch center. Prepare several seedless watermelon slice cutouts and cut out a supply of paper seeds. Program each slice with a different math fact answer. Then, for each slice, label five or six seeds with corresponding math facts. Code the backs of the cutouts for self-checking and, if desired, laminate the pieces for durability. Store the cutouts in a resealable plastic bag. Place the bag and one paper plate per watermelon slice in a basket. Set the basket at a center. A student lays each watermelon slice on a paper plate. Then she arranges the seeds on the corresponding slices. To check her work, she flips the seed cutouts. Delicious!

Lisa Strieker—Gr. 3, St. Paul Elementary, Highland, IL

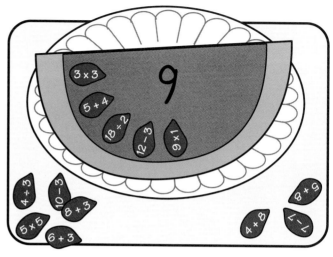

Hurray for Arrays!

Modeling multiplication builds a solid understanding of the multiplication concept. Label a class supply of cards with different fact problems. Place the cards, cereal pieces, glue, crayons, and sturdy paper at a center. A student selects a fact card. Then she makes and labels an array that models the problem and reveals its answer.

Sally Wallace—Gr. 3, O'Neill Elementary, O'Neill, NE

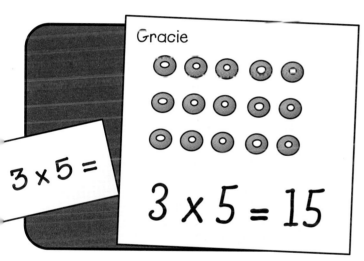

Delectable Division

Candy eggs lend a manipulative flair to **division** in this tasty math center. Partially fill five disposable bowls with cellophane grass, and fill an additional bowl with 30 foil-covered chocolate eggs. Also label a set of colorful, egg-shaped cutouts with division facts that have a divisor of five or less, and a dividend of 30 or less. (Depending on your students' abilities, include some problems with remainders.) Program the cutouts for self-checking and laminate them for durability. Place the bowls and the egg cutouts at a center. A student selects a cutout, reads the fact, and sets out as many grass-filled bowls as the divisor. To solve the fact, she takes the dividend in candy eggs and divides the eggs equally into the bowls. She places any leftover eggs (the remainder) to the side. Then she flips the cutout to check her work. If her answer is correct, she places the candy eggs back into their bowl. If her answer is incorrect, she adjusts her candy calculation before she returns the candy. The student continues in this manner until each division fact has been solved. If desired place a basket of candy eggs on your desk and invite each student who completes the center to treat herself to a candy egg from the basket!

Amy Polcyn—Substitute Teacher
South Lyon Community Schools, South Lyon, MI

Flavorful Fractions

This math center makes learning about **fractions** a sweet treat! For each student, place 12 miniature flavored marshmallows in a resealable plastic bag, making certain that each bag contains all four colors and no more than eight of any one color. Store the bags in a decorated container; then place the container, crayons, pencils, and student copies of page 158 at a center. Each student chooses a bag of marshmallows from the container and uses it to complete the reproducible activity. After a student has had a classmate verify his work, he eats his marshmallows in fractional portions! Mmmm, that ⁵⁄₁₂ of marshmallows was delicious!

Pam Williams—Gr. 3, Dixieland Elementary, Lakeland, FL

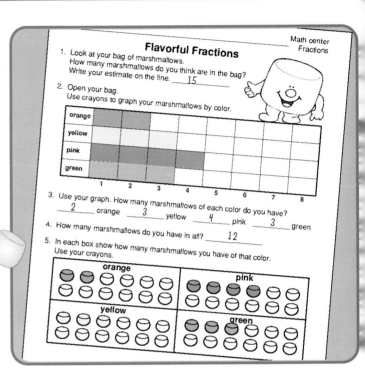

Fishing for Fractions

Reel in plenty of **fraction practice** at this tasty math center! In a clean container, mix a six-ounce package of cheddar fish-shaped crackers with similarly sized packages of pretzel and pizza fish-shaped crackers. Make a cracker code like the one shown. Then place the code, the container of crackers, napkins, a ¼-cup measurer, pencils, and student copies of page 159 at a center. A student places one-quarter cup of crackers on an unfolded napkin. Next, he sorts the crackers and completes the reproducible activity. When his work is finished, he eats his catch!

Melanie J. Miller
Nashport, OH

Fraction Creatures

These fun creatures familiarize students with **fractions**—and at the same time, challenge students to think creatively. Place a large supply of one-inch construction paper squares in assorted colors, black fine-tipped markers, a supply of 12" x 18" sheets of drawing paper, and glue at a center. A student folds a sheet of paper in half and in half again; then he unfolds his paper. At the top of each resulting quadrant, he writes a fraction with a denominator of four or less and a color word that describes some of the paper squares at the center. Each quadrant must be labeled differently. Then, in each quadrant, he uses the available supplies to create a creature that represents the quadrant's programming. For example, a creature created in a quadrant labeled "²⁄₃ blue" would be made with three paper squares—two of them blue. Fractions have never been more fun!

Belinda Darnall Vose—Gr. 1, Evergreen Elementary, Ocala, FL

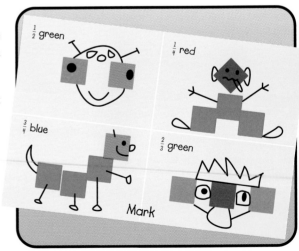

Shapely Creations

This hands-on activity familiarizes students with a variety of **shapes**—and at the same time, challenges students to think creatively. Place a set of attribute blocks, pencils, crayons or markers, and a supply of blank paper at a center. A student creates a desired picture by arranging the attribute blocks on a sheet of blank paper. When he is satisfied with his work, the student uses a pencil to trace around each block before he removes it from his paper. Then he colors his shapely creation!

Peggy Seibel—Gr. 2
St. Mary's School
Ellis, KS

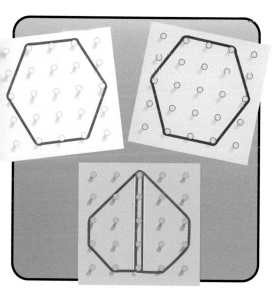

Geoboard Fun

Reinforce congruency and symmetry with these Geoboard partner activities. Place two Geoboards and several rubber bands at a center. To reinforce congruency, each partner needs a Geoboard and one or more rubber bands. One partner makes a desired shape on a Geoboard; then the other partner makes a congruent shape on his Geoboard. As soon as the students agree that their shapes are congruent, they switch roles and repeat the activity. Challenge each twosome to create a predetermined number of congruent shapes.

For practice with symmetry, one partner uses a rubber band to create a line of symmetry on one Geoboard. Then, working together on this Geoboard, one partner creates a desired shape on one side of the symmetry line. Next, the other partner arranges his rubber band on the board so that a symmetrical shape is created. As soon as the students agree that the shape is symmetrical, they switch roles and repeat the activity. Challenge each twosome to create a predetermined number of symmetrical shapes.

Peggy Seibel—Gr. 2
St. Mary's School
Ellis, KS

Trick or Treat!

Here's a sweet way to shape up your students' **geometry skills!** Fill a plastic jack-o'-lantern with individually wrapped candies in a variety of geometric shapes (such as cubes, cones, cylinders, spheres, and boxes). Consider choices such as caramel candies, Hershey's Kisses, miniature Tootsie Roll candies, Smarties candies, Starburst fruit chews, sour balls, and chocolate balls. Place the container of candy, a class supply of paper lunch bags, and crayons at a center. Also post a laminated sign, like the one shown, that can be reprogrammed each day with guidelines for filling a trick-or-treat bag. A student decorates a paper bag, reads the guidelines, and fills her bag accordingly. After a classmate verifies her work, she chooses one piece of her candy to eat; then she takes her remaining candy home.

Shelly Lanier, Reeds Elementary, Lexington, NC

Place these candies in your bag:

2 cylinders
1 sphere
4 cones
3 cubes
1 box

The Heart of Measurement

Students get to the heart of **measurement** at this seasonal center. Draw an assortment of premeasured lines inside a large heart cutout (a candy heart is the unit of measure). Number the lines and create an answer key. Laminate the heart and the answer key for durability. Place the heart, the answer key, a container of conversation hearts, pencils, and a supply of paper at a center. Using the candy hearts, the student measures each line and the perimeter of the heart to the nearest candy heart; then she writes her answers on her paper. She then uses the answer key to check her work. If desired, keep a container of conversation hearts on your desk and reward each child who completes the center with a handful of candy hearts.

Melissa Jo Owen—Gr. 3, Baty Elementary, Del Valle, TX

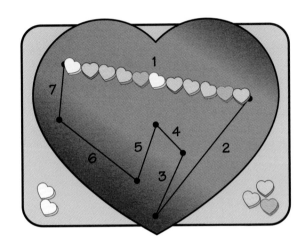

Scheduling Time

Here's a kid-pleasing activity that integrates **telling time and writing.** Place a clock stamp, a stamp pad, pencils, crayons, and a supply of blank paper at a center. A student titles her paper "A Perfect Saturday" and then stamps a column of clock faces down the left edge of the paper as shown. She programs the first clock to show the time she'll get out of bed. To the right of the clock she writes the matching analog time in crayon, and then she uses a pencil to describe what she plans to do at that time. She programs and labels the remaining clocks on her paper to show the activities she'd schedule for her perfect day. Display the completed schedules, and plenty of time-related conversations will follow!

Stacie Stone Davis
Lima, NY

For Good Measure

Students size up their **measurement skills** at this center. On individual cards write measurement-related questions that can be solved in the classroom. Consider questions like, "How many inches wide is the door?" and "Which weighs more—the red marker or the ruler?" Write student directions on a large card, and program the back of this card with an answer key. Laminate all the cards for durability. Place the question cards in a plastic two- or four-cup capacity container. Place the container, the direction card, a supply of paper, pencils, and the materials needed to answer the questions at a center. A student solves each measurement question and writes his answer on his paper. Then he uses the answer key to find out how his measurement skills measure up!

Tori Herrera—Gr. 3
Cook Elementary
Goshen, OH

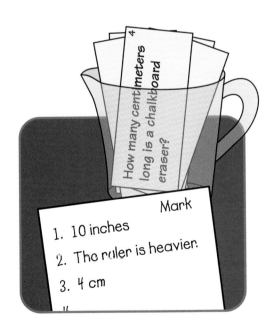

Coin Exchange

You can bank on **accurate coin exchanges** taking place at this partner center. Place a die and a container of imitation coins at a center. (For a game that concludes at 50¢, provide the following coins: ten pennies, three nickels, three dimes, three quarters, one half-dollar.) To play, partners take turns rolling the die. Each partner collects cents equal to the number he rolls. When a partner collects his coins, he evaluates his coin set. If he can exchange coins for a coin of greater value, he makes the trade. If a player overlooks a trade during his turn, his partner can point out the missed trade during his own turn and earn an extra roll of the die. The first player to collect 50¢ wins the game.

Anne M. Bosarge—Gr. 3
Lyman Elementary School
Richmond Hill, GA

Spending Money

Students go on a buying spree at this **money-skills** center! From discarded catalogs and store circulars, cut pictures of several kid-pleasing items and their prices. Glue each picture and its corresponding price on a construction paper card. Laminate the cards for durability. Next number five resealable plastic bags. In the bags place coin sets of varying values that can be used to purchase one or more of the pictured items. Place the bags, the picture cards, a supply of paper, and pencils at a center. A student writes the cash value of each coin set on her paper, followed by the name(s) of the item(s) she can buy with that amount of money. If desired, provide an answer key for students to check their work. Now, that's a bargain!

Trudy White—Gr. 2
Mayflower Elementary
Mayflower, AR

Cashing In

Money-counting skills are sure to profit at this partner center! Label the lids of an even number of empty film canisters with different money amounts. In a separate container place quarters, dimes, nickels, and pennies that can be used to make each money amount. Place the container of coins, the canisters, and a felt square at a center. Partner 1 selects a canister, places coins inside it that equal the programmed amount, and passes the canister to his partner. Partner 2 pours the coins onto the felt square and verifies the count. After the coins and empty canister are returned to their original locations, Partner 2 selects a different canister and the process is repeated. The partners continue in this manner until the coins in each canister have been counted and verified. Now, that's a center you can take to the bank!

Nell Roberts—Gr. 1, The Covenant School, Charlottesville, VA

Flavorful Fractions

1. Look at your bag of marshmallows.
   How many marshmallows do you think are in the bag?
   Write your estimate on the line. _____

2. Open your bag.
   Use crayons to graph your marshmallows by color.

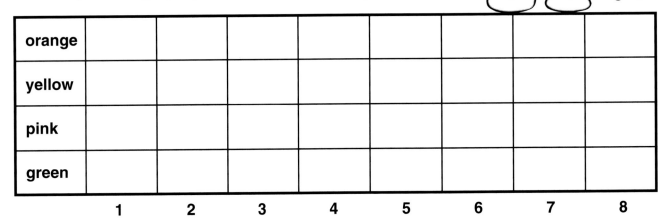

	1	2	3	4	5	6	7	8
orange								
yellow								
pink								
green								

3. Use your graph. How many marshmallows of each color do you have?

   _____ orange   _____ yellow   _____ pink   _____ green

4. How many marshmallows do you have in all? _____

5. In each box show how many marshmallows you have of that color.
   Use your crayons.

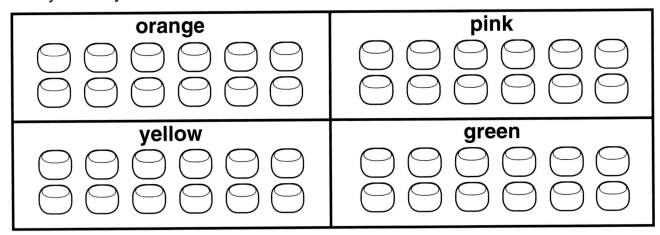

6. Study each box in Number 5. Write a fraction that describes it.

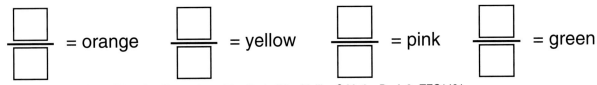

   $\dfrac{}{}$ = orange $\dfrac{}{}$ = yellow $\dfrac{}{}$ = pink $\dfrac{}{}$ = green

What a Catch!

Sort your catch of fish crackers.
Write a number to answer each question.

1. How many crackers in your catch are pizza? _____
2. How many crackers in your catch are cheddar? _____
3. How many crackers in your catch are pretzel? _____
4. How many crackers did you catch in all? _____

Remember! The bottom number is the total number of crackers in your catch.

Use the information above.
Write a fraction to answer each question.

5. What part of your catch is pizza?

6. What part of your catch is cheddar?

7. What part of your catch is pretzel?

The top number describes a part of the crackers.

On the lines, write a comparative sentence about each cracker.
(For example: I have more pizza crackers than pretzel crackers.)

8. Pizza: _____

_____

9. Cheddar: _____

_____

10. Pretzel: _____

_____

For Fraction Experts Only!
Write a fraction to answer each question.

11. What part of your catch is pizza and cheddar?

12. What part of your catch is pretzel and pizza?

13. What part of your catch is cheddar and pretzel?

14. What part of your catch is not cheddar?

Note to the teacher: Use with "Fishing for Fractions" on page 154.

Answer Keys

Page 7

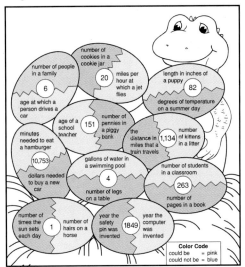

Bonus Box: Answers will vary.

Page 28

Order 1:	48 scoops	Order 7:	33 scoops
Order 2:	45 scoops	Order 8:	60 scoops
Order 3:	78 scoops	Order 9:	80 scoops
Order 4:	90 scoops	Order 10:	28 scoops
Order 5:	119 scoops	Order 11:	84 scoops
Order 6:	38 scoops	Order 12:	68 scoops

Page 31

Answers and their order may vary.

Star Cruiser	Cosmic Force
2, 5, 10	5, 9, 45
2, 4, 8	2, 4, 8
2, 9, 18	2, 3, 6
3, 6, 18	3, 10, 30
6, 6, 36	5, 6, 30
2, 3, 6	2, 10, 20
2, 6, 12	4, 9, 36
4, 3, 12	2, 5, 10

Bonus Box: The fact family for each number set found on each spacecraft should be provided.

Page 34

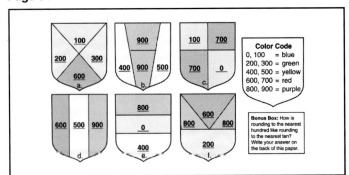

Bonus Box: Answers will vary. Students may respond that in both cases the number is rounded to the higher ten or hundred if the number being rounded is at least halfway between the tens or hundreds it falls between.

Page 46

Answers may vary. Possible answers are shown below.

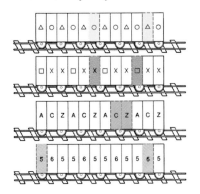

Page 104

Trail Mix

½ c. oat cereal
1 tsp. sunflower kernels
3 tsp. M&M's candies
¼ c. raisins
¾ c. honey-graham cereal
¼ c. pretzels

Page 124

1. the vampire
2. the ghost
3. the monster
4. the ghost
5. the vampire
6. the skeleton

Page 132

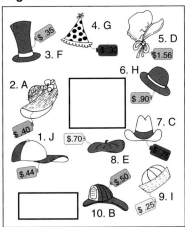

Page 141

1. 6 (a yellow star on six cars)
2. 2 (a red stripe on two cars)
3. 1 (a blue triangle on one car)
4. 2 (a purple square on two cars)
5. (an orange circle on one car)
6. a. $\frac{2}{12}$ or $\frac{1}{6}$
   b. $\frac{6}{12}$ or $\frac{1}{2}$
   c. $\frac{1}{12}$
   d. $\frac{1}{12}$
   e. $\frac{2}{12}$ or $\frac{1}{6}$

Bonus Box: Answers will vary.

Page 144

1. 52 + 16 = 68
2. 74 + 68 = 142
3. 10 + 16 = 26
4. 91 + 33 = 124
5. 45 + 10 = 55
6. 74 + 27 = 101
7. 91 + 16 = 107
8. 68 + 74 = 142
9. 27 + 27 = 54
10. 33 + 16 = 49
11. 91 + 52 = 143
12. 10 + 27 = 37
13. 27 + 45 = 72
14. 33 + 52 = 85